MW00882828

Celtic Advent —

Following an

Unfamiliar Path

Through Advent

By Christine Aroney-Sine

Cover Design by Hilary Horn
Cover Photo Christine Aroney-Sine

Poetry unless otherwise credited, by Christine Aroney-Sine

ISBN: 9798340329486
Imprint: Independently published

Dedication

To my brother Nick,
whose quiet presence in my life
always inspired, encouraged, and guided me.

Table of Contents

Introduction

Advent marks the beginning of the liturgical year. In the Western church it begins 4 Sundays before Christmas Day, but for Celtic and Orthodox Christians, it begins the evening of November 15th – forty days before Christmas Day. Celtic Christians always prayed and fasted for 40 days in preparation for any major life event, whether it be the planting of a new monastic center, the beginning of a new adventure as well as for preparation for Christmas and Easter.

In the Northern hemisphere Advent coincides with winter, once a dark, cold season in which everyone waited patiently for the coming of the light, but now ablaze with Christmas lights and streaming Christmas carols. In the Southern hemisphere where summer is in full swing, the sweltering Santas in their red suits, the artificial snow and reindeers, the long light filled evenings are a strident contrast to message of the season. Advent is meant to be a season of waiting, not a passive, idle and maybe boring waiting, but an active, soul searching and prayerful season. Yet these days, no matter where we live in the world it doesn't seem to fit. Something new needs to emerge to help guide us towards the birth of Christ.

It is 10 years now since I adopted the Celtic invitation to begin Advent on November 15th, 40 days before Christmas Day, before consumerism ramps up to a fever pitch and we become too distracted and overwhelmed by the busyness of the season to really take notice of what matters most. Advent is a time to prepare. We prepare to celebrate our remembrance of Christ's birth, 2000 years ago, we prepare to welcome him afresh as saviour in our lives and anticipate his return at the end of time when the fullness of God's redemption will be revealed and all creation will be made new.

As I prepare for Advent this year, I find myself caught in the tension between the familiar symbols of Nativity scenes, Christmas trees and

7

carol singing, and the desire for something unfamiliar which would jar me into fresh perspectives on the story of Jesus' birth and the revelations we receive from the humans, animals and angels that played important parts in it. It's these new perspectives that continue to grow my faith and draw me closer to God.

Once again, I was reminded of Heidi Haverkamp's suggestion in her devotional *Advent in Narnia*, that C.S. Lewis by placing Christianity into another world, makes it unfamiliar again and therefore opens our eyes, our hearts and our spirits to new aspects of a familiar story, that can therefore transform our lives in unexpected ways. She comments: "He gives us the chance to feel a new found wonder at the depths of God's love, the power of Christ's grace and the totality of his sacrifice, and the wonder of a world infused with the Holy Spirit." Surely that is what Advent is meant to be about - a season to reenter the wonder of our Creator and the incredible story of vulnerability, love, renewal and transformation that is revealed through the birth of Christ into our world, to gain fresh perspectives and move us onward towards the triune God.

Celtic Advent provides that same unfamiliarity for me. We don't know how the early Celtic Christians practiced Advent. This was in the days before nativity scenes, Advent wreaths, Christmas pageants and carol singing as we know them. It was certainly a time before commercialism and consumption formed the centre of our celebrations. We enter Celtic Advent with a blank canvas which opens up all kinds of new possibilities for the ways we celebrate.

There is a certain wildness to Celtic Christianity that is reflected in the lives of these "holy wanderers" who saw themselves as guests of the world, often taking long journeys to unknown destinations, relying on the spirit of God to lead them. There is so much that we can learn from this ancient future tradition whose followers lived lightly on this earth without becoming attached to possessions or place. They believed all of life was a pilgrimage, a journey towards God in which every experience and every encounter provided opportunity to both represent and learn about God.

There are several aspects of Celtic Christianity that I think are particularly pertinent to the Advent and Christmas season.

First, I love Scottish theologian, Prof John Macquarrie's observation that 'the Celt was very much a God-intoxicated person whose life was embraced on all sides by the divine Being."[1] I long for that same intoxication and intimacy with God where the awareness of God is present in every moment and every thing. There seems no better season than Advent to explore this deeper intimacy and spiritual intoxication.

Second, the Celts were very keen on what they called "peregrinatio" or holy wandering, the desire to travel to the place of one's resurrection and to experience personal resurrection not only in heaven, but also on earth. They did not go in search of God so much as to find a place where the presence of God, already active, could be nourished and expressed in service to others.[2]

Think of the journeys of Advent. Mary, after her encounter with an angel and revelation of her pregnancy journeys to see Elizabeth. Mary and Joseph journey to Bethlehem for the birth of the baby and then into Egypt to escape Herod. Last but not least, the Magi journey from a far country to see the infant Jesus. Though they may know the destination towards which that are moving, they are very much on an unknown journey of discovery, one that will lead them towards resurrection into a new life.

Third, for Celtic Christians creation was translucent, allowing us glimpses of the glory of God. The earth and its wonders provided the key not just to establishing the existence of God but also to learning about our Creator. This was no pantheistic worship of the elements but rather a dynamic picture of God's active presence in creation. God animates and charges all things with divine energy and they reflect and respond to God's creative presence and sustaining love. God's hands don't simply encircle and protect the earth and all it contains, God also quickens, enlivens and inspires it so God's existence can be confirmed through contemplation of the beauty and order of the natural world.

I love the way that Jan Blencowe expresses this in her article *Celtic Advent, A Little Bit Longer, A Little Bit Wider,*[3]:

"In Celtic Advent I think we have the opportunity to explore connection and communication with nature. We can come to know both the manifestations themselves, trees, stones etc. but also the spirit of those

things..... This deep connection to nature allows Celtic Advent to be primarily celebrated and contemplated through the natural world. Nature awaits the arrival of divinity, which will incarnate in it, and change it forever. This receiving of divinity includes what we receive in our own souls as well."

In our urban oriented society we forget that the events of Advent and Christmas revolved around and should not be separated from the natural world. Animals surrounded Jesus at his birth, shepherds, watching their flocks were visited by angelic hosts. All of it was set in small rural villages where life and nature interacted on a daily basis.

Fourth, one of the most demanding and often costly tasks undertaken by the Celtic monasteries was that of hospitality. They believed hospitality was not only meant to be a custom in their homes, they believed it was also a key into the kingdom of God. The guest house or hospitium, often occupied the best site within the monastic community and though the monks might live on bread and water visitors would often receive the best of food and drink. The monastery at Derry is said to have fed a thousand hungry people each day. Brigid who presided over the monastery at Kildare often made butter for visitors. Tradition has it that when churning the butter Brigit would make thirteen portions – twelve in honour of the apostles and an extra one in honour of Christ which was reserved for guests and the poor.

Advent and Christmas are stories of hospitality. Elizabeth welcomed Mary when she fled from her home. Joseph's family, I believe welcomed Mary into their home at Jesus birth and then in an incredible extension of hospitality also embraced the shepherds, the most despised of society, and the Magi, foreigners, probably Gentiles not Jews, from afar.

Fifth, Celtic Christianity revolved around the monastery, not the local parish church. This strongly monastic character produced a model of ministry that was communitarian rather than individualistic. *"Ministry in all aspects, liturgical, pastoral, evangelistic, educational was not the solitary individualistic task it so often is today. It was rather undertaken by teams of men and women, ordained and lay, who lived together in community and operated from a common central base from which they went out among the people preaching, teaching, baptizing, administering the sacraments, caring for the sick and burying the dead."*[4]

"These monastic communities were open to a constant stream of visitors, pilgrims and penitents. They were intimately involved in the affairs of the world and the lives of the people they served. The monks were not just concerned with the spiritual wellbeing of the communities they served but also with their intellectual and physical wellbeing. They were also in many ways the keepers of culture and tradition, not just copying the Psalms and Gospels but also writing down stories, songs, and poems and preserving myths and legends for posterity."[5]

The Advent and Christmas stories are about community as well. First there is family. Elizabeth is Mary's cousin, John is Jesus' cousin, Jesus is born in a family home in Bethlehem, but there is a broader community too that is essential to the story of Jesus' birth. The excluded ones - the shepherds and the non-Jewish Magi are welcomed into that home, the angels, the community of heaven who appear both as individuals and a huge singing chorus are all part of the gospel story of Jesus' birth. This community extended throughout the ages to embrace all who follow Christ.

Those angels open us to another important element of Celtic Christianity that is seen throughout the Advent and Christmas story, the belief that only a thin veil separates this world from the next. They took seriously Hebrews 12:1 "Seeing we are compassed about with so great a cloud of witnesses" and had an almost physical sense of the great company of heaven which surrounded God, embracing not just saints and friends who had died but the whole host of angels and other heavenly powers. When you raised your eyes to heaven you raised them to a vast host. The Celtic Christian at prayer was consciously a member of the great company that stretched from the persons of the Trinity through the powerful angelic throngs to the risen saints. They were regarded very much as friends and companions in this world and addressed almost as one would neighbours or members of the family.

There is a very strong sense in the Advent and Christmas story that the veil between heaven and earth is thin. A whole host of heavenly beings surround and interact with not only the Holy family but with all who enter the story - John's father receives a vision, the Magi are led by a star, the shepherds respond to an angelic host. If ever we are aware of the thinness of the veil, it is as we enter into the Advent story.

Jean McLachlan Hess in her *Journey to the Manger with Patrick and Friends* uses God and Holy Spirit for the additional two weeks of Celtic Advent. She points out that in Celtic Christianity all three persons of the Trinity are important. They are never separated one from one another,[6] but embraced as a family and each family unit, be it family, clan or tribe was seen as an icon of the Trinity. The Trinity was a very real presence in all aspects of life and creation, and an almost tangible comforter and protector who could ward off evil forces. Hess explains that Celtic Advent is designed to invite Emmanuel - *God the Trinity with us* - to travel with us, to be our navigator through the smooth and rough terrain of the season.

I love this idea but decided instead, in this devotional, to use *journey* and *hospitality* for the initial two weeks preceding the traditional themes of Hope, Peace, Joy and Love. Journey because Advent is an invitation to journey, to join with God as we move towards the birth of Christ. Hospitality partly because American Thanksgiving usually falls during this second week of Celtic Advent and our celebrations always seem to revolve around hospitality - both the need to be generous in our hospitality towards others and gratitude for God's hospitality toward us.

The sky's the limit as far as themes for each week of Celtic Advent are concerned. You don't even need to use the 4 traditional themes, though it is easier as most of our churches will embrace these. Perhaps you too would like to allow your imagination to flow as you prayerfully consider what themes you would like to choose for each of the weeks ahead.

I mentioned above that Celtic Advent traditionally begins on November 15th but it always helps to have a couple of days beforehand to prepare so this devotional begins on November 13th, which also rounds out the season of Advent to six weeks. Each day we will begin our journey with some thoughts from the Celtic tradition or a specific Celtic saint. Some like Columba, Brigid, Hilda and Patrick will weave their stories throughout the six weeks. Others we will only encounter once.

Each day ends with a short reflection for action, and a prayer. Some of the prayers I have written myself, some are from that wonderful repository of Celtic prayers the Carmina Gadelica. These prayers are the basis for our response each day to the stories we read. However be warned. I love to mess with traditions and so will throw in a few non Celtic adventures too, like a trip to Abuna Yemata Guh in Ethiopia.

Some of the reflections invite you to journal, or engage in activities that take you out of your sacred space and into God's world. You might like to prepare a travel kit for the adventure - your journal to both write and sketch in, colouring pencils, pens or paint pens, as well as other items that appeal to your form of creativity.

So lets get going and begin our journey together.

God be with us on our journey,
Guide us on the way.
Keep us free from all distractions,
Give us strength and safety too.
Grant us grace for each encounter,
And patience with delays.
May our hearts be ever open
To new adventures and friendships that will form.
May we be stretched by new ideas,
And wisdom from above.
Three in One,
One in Three,
Keep us searching for your presence
In everything we do.
May we be transformed by all that happens,
And return home ever changed.

Week 1 — Holy Wanderings

November 13th — Set Your Heart in the Right Direction

The true light that shines on all people
was coming into the world.
The light was in the world,
and the world came into being through the light,
but the world didn't recognize the light.
The light came to his own people,
and his own people didn't welcome him.
But those who did welcome him,
those who believed in his name,
he authorized to become God's children, (John 1:9-12 CEB)

"As we begin this journey of Advent start by setting your heart in the right direction"[7]. As I read this reflection in David Cole's excellent Celtic Advent devotional a few years ago, I realized how much I need to set my own heart in the right direction. Focusing on Advent and the coming of Christ as the intention of my heart and soul isn't always easy but I know it is extremely important.

I use the few days before Celtic Advent to dream and imagine what I want my sacred space to look like for the season. The purpose of Advent is to lead us towards the Christ Child and the transformation his light within us brings. Lots of candles is the first thing that comes to mind. Light in the darkness, brightness to lead us toward the one true light. I usually begin by setting up a circle of light around my sacred space. I started this practice several years ago with a few electric candles on my desk and the cabinet that sits behind me, but each year the number of candles has grown. Now when I sit in the dark and light my candles each morning I am surrounded by a magnificent circle of about 40 candles that embrace me and draw me into the comforting presence of God.

I also like to set up an Advent wreath and since I embraced Celtic Advent have enjoyed experimenting with what that could look like. It's very hard to find a six candled Advent wreath. Some years I set up a small garden in which I place a candle of different colours for each week of Celtic Advent then replace them with half a dozen white candles at Christmas reflecting the fact that for me Christ's light is too bright to be represented by a single candle. In other years I set up a green wreath and placed my 6 candles - five purple and one pink - in a circle, leaving space for the Christ candle at the centre. Last year I purchased a centerpiece with six candleholders in it, decorated the votive holders with Celtic designs and transformed it into a Celtic Advent wreath. I placed a small platform in the centre on which a small manger scene stands. I also arranged all my Celtic crosses around my space, interspersed with my candles. Evidently the Celtic monasteries were often surrounded by a circle of crosses as a symbol of protection and I really find comfort in this addition to my space.

Advent is not a journey we embark on alone. I love to celebrate this season in our small intentional community, the Mustard Seed House. At our first Advent community meal, we light our beautiful Celtic designed oil lamp and each person places a tea light in a circle around it. We share Celtic prayers and why we are attracted to Celtic Christianity. I perform a similar ritual each week throughout the Advent season, possibly adding some Celtic drawing or rock painting exercises one week. I look forward to this fun way to celebrate our extended Advent season.

At the beginning of traditional Advent I pull out my icons and other Advent images. We purchase our Christmas tree and set up our traditional Advent wreath on the dining room table. It is a delight to light the appropriate candles each morning as we eat breakfast and reflect on the season.

I enjoy greatly applying my imagination and creativity to the season. It adds meaning and purpose as I set my heart in the right direction, following Jesus towards the manger.

Reflection

Sit in your sacred space. Read through this prayer three times, imagining the God who encircles you as you begin this journey. Sit still and breathe in the breath that enlivens you. Draw an imaginary circle around you and sit in the comfort of the God who walks this journey with you.

Celtic Advent and the symbols we use in it are intended to lead us to the Christ Child, our remembrance of his birth 2000 years ago, his abiding presence in our lives today, and our expectation of his return at the end of the age when his presence will restore all things. What symbols help you focus during the season of Advent? How could you incorporate them into an altar or sacred space that will remain with you throughout the season?

Today, we stand in God's circle of light,
Breathing in, breathing out.
Today we stand in God's circle of light,
Light before, light behind,
Light on left, light on right,

Light buried deep within.
Today, we stand in God's circle of light,
With friends and family, neighbours and strangers,
With all the people of the world.
Together we stand in God's everlasting light.
Encircled, embraced,
United into one family,
From every nation and culture and creed.
Let this circle hold us,
Let this circle sustain us,
Let this circle surround us,
With the bright and shining presence
Of the Eternal One,
Who leads us into light.

November 14th — Circling Through Celtic Advent

Because of our God's deep compassion,
the dawn from heaven will break upon us,
to give light to those who are sitting in darkness
and in the shadow of death,
to guide us on the path of peace." (Luke 1:78, 79 CEB)

One of my favourite yearly celebrations is Looking for Circles Day on November 2nd. I go out into my garden and walk around my neighbourhood looking for the circles hidden in so many aspects of creation. Circles are everywhere. The whorls of our fingerprints and the rings that encircle them, the spiral patterns in leaves or on a special rock, the wheels of cars, and, of course, the mysterious crop circles are a few examples. Some of the circles around us are perfect, some are in the form of spirals, some are broken by scars and damage. Yet in all, the circular pattern is discernible.

Circles were very significant to the Celts. As I already mentioned, it was felt that a circle with no break was a symbol of eternal life, a complete whole affording no access to the devil. It was a symbol of unity, togetherness and purity.

There are two kinds of Celtic symbols - the Celtic Cross and Celtic knots that are based on a circular pattern. Celtic knots are complete loops that have no start or finish and could be said to represent eternity whether this means loyalty, faith, friendship or love. Only one thread is used in each design which symbolizes how life and eternity are interconnected. Both Illustrated Bible manuscripts, like the spectacular Book of Kells, and Celtic crosses are often decorated with Celtic knots. The Trinity knot is arguably the best known Celtic knot and is also called the Triquetra. Composed of three equal interlaced arcs with a never-ending unbroken line, representing equality, eternity & unity, its points are said to represent the Holy Trinity of the Creator, Redeemer & Breath of God though this cannot be verified as historically accurate. However it does seem that many of these interlaced designs reflected the Celtic belief in life's interconnectedness and continuity.

Celtic crosses are a unique type of cross in that they incorporate the circle at their heart. Some have suggested that this circle depicts the wreath given to military heroes in Rome showing Christ's victory over the forces of evil. Others see it as a halo representing the holiness of the one who died there. Still others think the circle was a pagan sign depicting the sun or the earth, the natural world. By superimposing the sign on the cross, the Celts expressed their view that the revelation of God comes to us through the natural world and in the person of Jesus Christ. We need both to get the full picture, so the two are bound together with the circle at the intersection of the natural and the spiritual realms[8]. The Celtic saints had a powerful sense of the unity of the whole created order and believed that God is always at work making all things whole. This story is hidden within all our hearts and within all of creation. We rejoice with God's creation where the circle is ever present and yet often distorted, disfigured or scarred. We rejoice too with those who have borne witness to this dream of wholeness throughout the centuries, living their lives to bring healing, freedom and abundance to the oppressed, the hurting and the abandoned.

The high crosses of the Celts like the Muiredach's High Cross at Monasterboice and the Cross of the Scriptures at Clonmacnoise usually feature amazingly detailed carvings of scenes from the bible and were evidently used as teaching stations. I can only imagine the hundreds, if not thousands of people who stood at the base of these crosses and gazed up the circles, learning about the story of Jesus, his birth, life, death and resurrection, receiving in him the promise of the One in whom this circle of wholeness will be completed. It is God's promise of wholeness and the completion of the healing both of creation and of all humankind that the circle represents, that we all long for and look forward to each time we celebrate this story.

As I settle into Celtic Advent, and use Celtic images to help guide us I am aware that we, too, stand with those who stood before these Celtic crosses, learning and teaching. We are joining a great cloud of holy witnesses who have gone before us. I not only surround myself with crosses and candles in a circle, but also like to use the circling prayers, like those used by the Celtic saints. These provide that same sense of completeness and protection from the devil that the circle of crosses seemed to. They helped set boundaries, sometimes in the form of an imaginary circle, sometimes as a real circle, like the ring of crosses around a monastery.

As we move towards Christmas, we all need the type of boundaries and strength that the Celtic circle and the circling prayers it inspired, provide. I cannot describe the depth of comfort and sustenance they bring me. God's encircling presence and protection is profound, not just physically. I sense God encircling my mind and my heart embracing me with divine light and presence.

Reflection

Walk around your house or neighborhood and see how many circles you can find. Take photos or make a list and spend time reflecting on God's wholeness revealed in the world around you as you begin your Advent journey.

Now work on a circling prayer (Caim Prayer), using the template below.

(Caim Prayer)

Circle me Lord,
Keep joy within, and fear without
keep peace within and hate without,
Keep love within and despair without.
Circle me Lord.

What things do you want within the circle of God's protection? What do you want to push outside?

Repeat the prayer above using your own words from the list you made. Keep— — within and — — without.

Circle us lamb of God
abide within our hearts.
Circle us word of God
speak through our lips.
Circle us dove of God
grant peace along our path.
Circle us with your witnesses.
Those who have gone before.
Circle us with your wholeness.
The way on which we tread
Circle us with your love.
Let it enfold our journey

November 15th — Journeying with All the Saints

The Word became flesh
and made his home among us.
We have seen his glory,
glory like that of a father's only son,
full of grace and truth. (John1:14 CEB)

Celtic Christians loved to journey. They seemed to have an innate yearning to explore the unknown, a wanderlust that took many of them throughout Europe and across the seas. All of us have heard of St. Brendan the Voyager, but he was not the only Celtic Christian to journey far to spread the faith. Beginning with St. Patrick, they chose a way of life that took many of them far from home. They faced what was known as "white martyrdom" living for years away from homes and family they loved for the sake of the gospel. The Celts had a specific word, *hiraeth,* for the extreme yearning for home associated with this latter form of martyrdom; because of their deep love of family it was considered the hardest form of martyrdom to endure.[9]

When Tom and I were in Switzerland a number of years ago we came across a small Celtic chapel on the banks of Lake Thun. It was planted by unnamed Irish monks who established it in the 8th century. On another occasion we visited Würzburg Germany in time for the Feast Day of St. Killian, a 7th century Irish monk, who is the patron saint of the city. When we visited Assisi we discovered that Francis of Assisi was thought to have spent time in a Celtic monastery in Bobbio in Northern Italy. It is speculated that it greatly influenced his life and his love of animals.

It is thought that these Celtic wanderers chose this way of life not just because of their deep devotion to Christ, but also because of their genuine appreciation of God's beautiful creation and their own desire to see holy places and meet people different from themselves. They believed that these journeys - known as *peregrinatio* - brought unexpected blessings, incredible intimacy with God and the healing of body and soul. [10] Those that survived to return home would have had much wisdom and many insights to share about their new experiences and would have passed these on through mentoring relationships to those they left behind. I love how Norwegian Arne Bakken expresses the richness of this type of experience. "the old pilgrims never returned to their own land and homestead without having lost a prejudice and gained a new idea instead. This is an attitude of life which constantly seeks new enlightenment, carries with it new won experiences and allows life to be influenced by it."[11]

Advent too is about journeying and the willingness to leave behind the familiar and the comfortable to explore the unexpected and unfamiliar. It is about opening our eyes to new enlightenment and new ideas. It is an invitation to join with Mary, Joseph and so many followers of Christ throughout the centuries in following God towards the manger and the birth of Jesus Christ, a journey that always has new things to teach us about life and faith.

Reflection

This prayer of St. Brendan is a great one to reflect on as we begin our journey together. Read through the prayer several times. Close your eyes and allow it to sink into your heart. What is God saying to you as you begin this journey?

What other resources will assist your journey? Are there books you want to carry with you? Are there companions who will help bear your burdens and support you on the way? As you reflect on your own life, how might God be calling you to leave the familiar? You may be experiencing change or transition in your life. How might God be speaking through the unfamiliar, or accompanying you during times of change?

Help me to journey beyond the familiar
and into the unknown.
Give me the faith to leave old ways
and break fresh ground with You.
Christ of the mysteries, I trust You
to be stronger than each storm within me.

I will trust in the darkness and know
that my times, even now, are in Your hand.
Tune my spirit to the music of heaven,
and somehow, make my obedience count for You.[12]

November 16th — Wandering with Brendan

The angel said, "Don't be afraid, Mary. God is honoring you. Look! You will conceive and give birth to a son, and you will name him Jesus. He will be great and he will be called the Son of the Most High. (Luke 1:30-32 CEB)

St. Brendan the Navigator is one of my favourite Celtic saints, partly, I think, because I spent 12 years of my life living on board a ship. I know how terrifying it can be to be tossed by storms, and swept close to rocks. I know what it feels like to sail to unfamiliar places anticipating new experiences that would draw me closer to my travelling companions and towards God. And that was in a large diesel fueled modern ship. I can hardly picture myself in the place of Brendan... standing at the wooden jetty, peering down at a feeble looking boat or curragh, that he himself had made with unseasoned wood and leather, smeared in animal grease to seal it from the waves. In the bottom of the craft lay a roll of leather, there to patch the unavoidable leaks and tears the journey would bring. And crammed into that boat are the 14 monks who will be his companions for the next seven years, staring out across the ocean toward the horizon, the edge of their known world, into the unknown. Maybe there are distant lands across the sea, maybe there is nothing, only God knows!

Deep inside you hear a call that says "Set sail into the unknown, step off the edge of your world and come with me into mine." That is just what these adventurous men did. Stirred by that wanderlust for knowledge and adventure, it is believed that Brendan set sail with a group of monks from the Dingle peninsula in Ireland in their curragh in search of the Isle of the Blessed.

There are many spectacular myths and legends that surround their voyage. They are said to have visited the northern Isles of Scotland, the Faeroe islands, Iceland and eventually Newfoundland. Legend has it that just before Easter one year, they built a paschal fire on what appeared to be a small island. When it moved they realized that it was actually an enormous whale. Seven years later they returned home with flora and fauna that was neither Irish, nor European. What we know for certain is that they drifted free at the mercy of the wind and the whim of the waves, in the will of God.

I think that Mary and Joseph, Elizabeth and Zechariah must all have felt a little like these monks as they began their unknown journey with God towards the birth of Christ. Spectacular visits from angels and then nothing for nine months. Cast adrift as it seemed to fend for themselves as they waited for the birth of a child who would change their lives and our world forever. They too must have felt as though God had pushed them off into the unknown future with a very small and unreliable vessel to journey in. How often I wonder did Mary doubt the words the angel Gabriel spoke to her? How often did she run in fear for her life? Was that why she ran to Elizabeth after she found out she was pregnant? Was her cousin the safe person who provided a haven of comfort and support during those early days?

Reflection

What are the moorings in your life? Not the things that frustrate you, but the things you hold on to. The comforts which you cling to, the insecurities which cloud your willingness to sail into the unknown.

What are your dreams, the dreams which seem far too distant and unreachable. What are the visions you have that feel beyond your grasp, too vast? What are the big ideas which leave you stumped, no idea of how to even start? Take a few moments to ponder what would it take for you to reach for them, and set sail as Brendan and Mary did towards an unknown future.

Disturb us, O Lord
when we are too well-pleased with ourselves
when our dreams have come true because we dreamed too little,
because we sailed too close to the shore.
Disturb us, O Lord
when with the abundance of things we possess,
we have lost our thirst for the water of life
when, having fallen in love with time,
we have ceased to dream of eternity
and in our efforts to build a new earth,
we have allowed our vision of Heaven to grow dim.
Stir us, O Lord
to dare more boldly, to venture into wider seas
where storms show Thy mastery,
where losing sight of land, we shall find the stars.
In the name of Him who pushed back the horizons of our hopes
and invited the brave to follow.
Amen[13]

November 17th — Standing with Patrick

Mary got up and hurried to a city in the Judean highlands. She entered Zechariah's home and greeted Elizabeth. When Elizabeth heard Mary's greeting, the child leaped in her womb, and Elizabeth was filled with the Holy Spirit. (Luke 1: 39-41, CEB)

When we think of St. Patrick, it is not as a journeyer that we consider him and yet his travels defined who he was. Sometimes forced upon him, sometimes made voluntarily, the journeys he made throughout his life not only determined who he was as a follower of Jesus, but also strengthened and sustained him. As a youth he was captured by pirates and taken to Ireland as a slave where he remained for six years. His life as a shepherd was harsh, but it was here that he began to pray the prayers of his childhood and found in them the living Christ who he knew would never leave or forsake him. Finally, guided by inner voices and dreams, he escaped and returned home, but once again responded to a dream figure that told him to come back and walk with the Irish once more. His willingness to respond shows the strength of his faith and his dedication to the One he now followed.

His journey back was a circuitous one however. Feeling he was not well enough qualified for the task, he set out to visit Rome and pay his respects to the the head of the church. He crossed the sea and began his journey through Gaul but arriving in Auxerre, he met bishop Germanus, and spent many years with him growing in wisdom, knowledge and love of God. I wonder if this became a place of comfort and safety for him. Maybe the calling on his life began to fade from his memory. Maybe he hoped for a less dangerous life. Finally, however, he had another vision which prompted him to resume his journey back to Ireland.

Starting at Tara, the home of the High King of Ireland, he travelled extensively, spreading the good news of the gospel in spite of being attacked, beaten and at times put in irons. Evidently he was instrumental in converting thousands of people and planting dozens of churches and monasteries. Patrick is credited with incorporating traditional Irish symbols, rituals, and festivals into the Christian faith, creating a unique blend that laid the foundation for Ireland's distinct Christian identity.

I wonder as I consider Patrick's life if it was the same for Mary. We don't think of her as a journeyer and yet she spent much of her time after Jesus' conception travelling. She too faced many hazards on her journeys, from the possible threat to her life and that of her child because she was an unwed mother, to the rigours of a long journey when heavily pregnant, a trip to Jerusalem to dedicate Jesus on the eighth day and then the flight into Egypt with a young baby. Wow she was quite the traveller. How did her belief in the purposes of God grow and mature as she journeyed from the conception of Jesus to his birth and beyond?

Reflection

Patrick's determination in the face of adversity is reflected in St. Patrick's Breastplate which I have adapted here as a responsive reading. I can imagine Mary, Joseph, Elizabeth and all the personalities of the Advent story using such a prayer as they too faced the challenges of their journeys. Prayerfully read through it several times, allow the words to penetrate your heart and mind.

Reflect on times of adversity in your own life and how God accompanied you. Allow God to speak to you as you reflect. You might like to write your own version of the prayer, or respond to it through another form of creativity that appeals to you.

We bind unto ourselves today
the strong name of the Trinity,
By invocation of the same,
the Three in One and One in three.
We bind this day to us forever, by power of faith, Christ's Incarnation;
His baptism in the Jordan River; his death on cross for my salvation;
His bursting from the spiced tomb; His riding up the heavenly way;
his coming at the day of doom; We bind unto ourselves today.
We cast off the works of darkness,
And put on the armour of light,
Light before us and behind,
Light within and light without,
Light to guide and to lead us,
Let us clothe ourselves with Christ.
Christ behind us, Christ before us,
Christ beside us, Christ to win us,
Christ to comfort and restore me,
Christ beneath us, Christ above us,
Christ in quiet, Christ in danger,
Christ in hearts of all that love us,
Christ in mouth of friend & stranger,
Let us wrap ourselves with the belt of truth,
And strap on the breastplate of righteousness,
Let us clad our feet with the gospel of peace,
Place the helmet of salvation on our heads.
And take up the shield of faith.
Let us clothe ourselves with Christ.

We bind unto ourselves today, the power of God to hold and lead,
God's eye to watch, God's might to stay, God's ear to harken to our need,
The wisdom of our God to teach, God's hand to guide, and shield to ward,
The Word of God to give us speech, God's heavenly host to be our guard.
In the love of our Creator who shelters us,
In the light of our Companion who walks beside us,
In the power of the Comforter who dwells within us,
We place ourselves today.
Let us clothe ourselves with Christ.
We bind unto ourselves today the strong name of the Trinity,
By invocation of the same, the Three in One, the One in Three.
Of whom all nature hath creation, Eternal God, Spirit, Word;
Praise to the God of our salvation, Salvation is of Christ the Lord.

November 18th — Trusting with Ia

Mary said,
"With all my heart I glorify the Lord!
In the depths of who I am I rejoice in God my savior.
He has looked with favor on the low status of his servant.
Look! From now on, everyone will consider me highly favored
because the mighty one has done great things for me.
Holy is his name." (Luke 1:46-48 CEB)

St. Ia (also known as *Eia, Hia, Ive* or *Hya*) is the patron saint of the picturesque town of St. Ives in Cornwall, England. She was an Irish woman of noble birth, possibly a princess, who was deeply religious but like many women, not taken seriously by her male companions. Evidently Ia went to the seashore to depart for Cornwall with the monks Gwinear, Finger and Piala only to see their boat disappearing over the horizon. Fearing that she was too young for such a hazardous journey, she was grief-stricken and began to pray. As she prayed, she noticed a small leaf floating on the water and touched it with a rod to see if it would sink. As she watched, it grew bigger and bigger. Trusting God, she embarked upon the leaf and was carried across the Irish Sea, reaching Penwith in Cornwall before the others.

Ia became a disciple of St. Berwyn and was soon joined by St. Elwyn and 777 companions. She may also have made sojourns to Brittany, where Plouyé near Carhaix is named after her. Ia's presence in Penwith was not, however, universally popular. She was persecuted by the local ruler, King Teudur who eventually found her so troublesome that he had her murdered. She was buried at Porth Ia (St. Ives).

As I read Ia's story I was reminded of one of my childhood heroes, Gladys Aylward born in 1902, in London. Following a calling to go overseas as a Christian missionary, she was accepted by the China Inland Mission but eventually rejected because of her lack of progress in learning Chinese. Because she strongly believed God intended her to go to China, she spent her life savings on a train passage across Siberia to Yangcheng, which turned out to be more of an adventure than she anticipated. Russia and China were in an undeclared war. She was detained by the Russians but managed to evade them through local help and a lift from a Japanese ship. She then traveled across Japan, and took another ship to China. She helped govern The Inn of the Eight Happinesses and became a revered figure among the people, taking in orphans and adopting several herself. She also intervened in a volatile prison riot and advocated prison reform, risking her life many times to help those in need. In 1938, when the region was invaded by Japanese forces, Gladys led more than 100 orphans to safety over the mountains, despite being wounded and sick, personally caring for them. Her story is immortalized in the 1958 film The Inn of the Sixth Happiness which made an indelible impact on my young life.

Ia and Aylward, like so many other women of faith throughout the centuries trusted deeply in the God who led them. Their persistence in the face of what seemed to be insurmountable challenges was remarkable and a great lesson to all of us as we walk through Advent with that other remarkable woman, Mary. She too faced seemingly insurmountable obstacles and experienced remarkable visitations as she walked the journey God chose for her.

Reflection

Sit for a few minutes with your eyes closed. Imagine each of these intrepid women stepping out into the unknown, trusting God for the seeming impossible. Trusting God when the road ahead is shrouded in darkness isn't easy. Believing in the promises of God when the future holds seemingly insurmountable challenges can test anyone's faith. When was the last time you faced a challenging situation that taxed your strength and tested your faith? How did you respond? Who have been some of the women like Ia, Gladys and Mary in your life and what have you learned from them about what it means to trust God as we journey towards the manger?

God of all goodness and grace,
Let us learn to walk in the dark,
In places where light is dim,
And we cannot see.
Help us to move slowly
And not stumble,
Attentive to touch and sound and smell.
May we cherish
The intimacy of your inner voice,
And the gentle love of your guiding presence.
God of all life and wholeness,
Let us learn to walk in the dark,
Where every step needs trust,
And it takes faith to journey onwards.
Let us learn to see,
The inner glow of your light
Behind us, before us, around us,
Within us, in others and in our world.

November 19th — Exiled with Columba

Since Joseph belonged to David's house and family line, he went up from the city of Nazareth in Galilee to David's city, called Bethlehem, in Judea. He went to be enrolled together with Mary, who was promised to him in marriage and who was pregnant. While they were there, the time came for Mary to have her baby. (Luke 2: 4-6 CEB)

I love the tiny island of Iona off the west coast of Scotland. It is a spiritual home for my husband Tom and myself and we have enjoyed the privilege of visiting it on several occasions over our 32 years together. It was here that Irish born Columcille or Columba, as he is better known, settled after being exiled from Ireland following one of the bloodiest battles in Irish history. Born into a royal family in Donegal, Ireland in 521 A.D., he was a man of exceptional gifts who loved learning, poetry and the psalms but I think he was also pretty arrogant. He was accused of copying a book of psalms that belonged to another monk, probably one that was decorated with beautiful illustrations. The dispute erupted in an armed and blood battle. Columba's supporters fought and won, but three thousand men died in the conflict. Columba saw the destructiveness that his possessiveness and greed caused. Overcome with remorse he left his beloved country, fleeing into exile with twelve companions and determined to sail until he could no longer see Ireland. They landed on the small island of Iona where they established a monastery that would become the heart of the Celtic church. From there Columba travelled throughout Scotland, converting tribal chiefs and kings and establishing churches.

From the poetry and stories about Columba which survived, it seems he never got over his homesickness for Ireland, especially his beloved Derry. He made at least one journey back to Ireland, visiting his monks in Durrow and other monasteries, before he died on Iona in 597[14] As one who has not lived in her homeland of Australia for almost 50 years I can understand the longing of his heart for the home of his birth. One time I landed in Johannesburg, South Africa in the middle of the night. As we drove to the place we were staying the fragrant aroma of eucalyptus leaves overwhelmed me. I took deep breaths in and out. "It smells like home" I exclaimed! There is something special about the place we grew up in that pulls at our heart strings no matter how long our travels may keep us from it. It is an ache that is forever lodged in our hearts.

I wonder, if, as Mary travelled to Bethlehem and then later into Egypt, she felt that same longing for home that Columba did. It is possible she was born in Jerusalem but probably grew up in Nazareth. Yet from the time she conceived until long after Jesus was born she saw little of her birthplace. Did she wonder as she travelled into the hill country to spend time with her cousin Elizabeth if she would ever be able to return home without fear of being stoned? Did she suffer from homesickness on that journey to Bethlehem unsure of what kind of welcome she would receive from Joseph's family? Did she long for family and the comforts of Nazareth as together with Joseph and the baby Jesus she made her way as a refugee into exile in Egypt?

Reflection

Columba's life began with a vision when his mother dreamt that her son would be a great prophet destined to be the leader of innumerable souls. I wonder how much that vision sustained him and shaped his decisions as he was exiled to Iona and experienced redemption and renewal. Out of the ashes of failure he was strengthened to create a new community that would spread the gospel throughout Scotland, England and, through his followers, into Europe.

Mary's vision received from the angel Gabriel must have sustained her through her pregnancy and exile into Egypt too. Have you or someone you love had a vision about your future that you feel was a call from God? Close your eyes and return to a special place where you felt the nearness of God and were strengthened by that vision. Take time to reflect on how that shaped your life. How has it sustained you over the years?

Be Thou my vision, O Lord of my heart
Be all else but naught to me, save that Thou art
Be Thou my best thought in the day and the night
Both waking and sleeping, Thy presence my light.

Be Thou my wisdom, be Thou my true word
Be Thou ever with me, and I with Thee, Lord
Be Thou my great Father, and I Thy true son
Be Thou in me dwelling and I with Thee one.

Be Thou my breastplate, my sword for the fight;
Be Thou my whole armour, be Thou my true might;
Be Thou my soul's shelter, be Thou my strong tower,
O raise Thou me heavenward, great power of my power.

Riches I heed not, nor vain, empty praise
Be Thou mine inheritance, now and always
Be Thou and Thou only the first in my heart
O high King of heaven, my treasure Thou art.

High King of heaven, Thou heaven's bright sun
O grant me its joys, after victory is won;
Great Heart of my own heart, whatever befall,
Still be Thou my vision, O Ruler of all.[15]

Week 2 — Guests of the World

November 20th — Pilgrimage with Brendan & Columba

Those who put their strength in you are truly happy;
  pilgrimage is in their hearts.
As they pass through the Baca Valley,
  they make it a spring of water.
  Yes, the early rain covers it with blessings.
They go from strength to strength,
  until they see the supreme God in Zion. (Psalm 84:5-7 CEB)

I believe in pilgrimage, taking time out of our regular lives to go on a journey of discovery with God. In the practice of pilgrimage, my husband Tom and I have journeyed to Jerusalem, to Iona and Holy Island and visited St. Catherine's monastery near Mount Sinai in the Egyptian desert. On other occasions we have set aside special pilgrimage days to visit ancient churches, war memorials and monastic ruins. Pilgrimages have taught me to think as a pilgrim in regular life too. They encouraged me to take time to notice what God is doing around me and to see interruptions as gifts rather than a curse. They have taught me too to welcome all that comes to mind - be it thoughts, ideas, scenery or people.

Many scholars consider pilgrimage as the distinctive feature of Celtic Christianity. Celtic Christians embraced the story of Abraham and Sarah who left their home and country to travel into the unknown. These pioneers of the Hebrew race spent the rest of their lives living in tents, wandering with no permanent place to call home. Celts identified strongly with them. Their own origins started in Switzerland from which some ventured east into central Turkey, where they became known as Gauls. The region they settled in became known as Galatia. Some say that the Galatians addressed in Paul's letter were early Celtic people. Most however journeyed west into modern day France, in such numbers that it became known as Gaul. Julius Caesar pushed them further west onto Britain and eventually into the less desirable rugged Scottish highlands and across the narrow sea to Ireland.[16] It was this journeying that taught them to live lightly on the land and to regard themselves as guests of the world.

Celts were well aware that they lived literally at the edge of the known world. They saw no better way to give themselves fully to the God revealed in Jesus Christ than to leave their native land on pilgrimage. Some, like Brendan struck out into the unknown, in the spirit of Abraham and Sarah, trusting God to show them where they should go. Others, like Columba, left with more intentionality and a desire to share the gospel with those who'd not heard the message. Columba established monasteries at Durrow and Derry and numerous churches in Ireland before he was exiled and established a home base on Iona from which he and his fellow monks continued to travel, evangelizing, establishing churches and monasteries throughout Scotland, Northern England and into Europe. Their physical journey represented an inner journey to focus more intentionally on the presence of God.

Today people still go on pilgrimage. In fact it seems to be more popular than ever. Some go to Jerusalem to walk the places where Jesus walked and to see where the events of the Bible took place. Young people from all over the world journey to Taize[17], in France to sing and pray together and live in community. Others walk the Way of St. James in Spain to Santiago de Compostela, known as the Camino.[18] And still others visit the former Celtic monastic sites of Iona, Holy Island, Glendalough and the desolate Skellig Islands off the coast of Ireland.

These modern pilgrims seek to connect with God. They journey to "thin places" where heaven and earth seem to touch and where they can experience the divine presence. God speaks to us in the thin places of life, along the edges where life is less busy, less noisy and when we are less pre-occupied with the worries of everyday life. God speaks to us in community, because we need each other to grow and expand and process our faith. All of these things can happen on pilgrimage. We too can grow on and in our journey of faith by practicing pilgrimage!

Advent is a story of pilgrimage. Like Sarah and Abraham and the early Celts, Mary and Joseph were pushed out of their comfortable life and their home in Nazareth by God's call to be the earthly parents of the son of God. From the moment of her encounter with an angel and the revelation of her pregnancy Mary seems to have been on the move and

43

in each place she is dependent on the hospitality of others to protect and support her and her unborn child. First she journeys to the hill country, about 90 miles away, to see Elizabeth. She must only have been back in Nazareth for a couple of months when she sets out with Joseph on the journey to Bethlehem and the birth of Jesus. Then an even longer journey into Egypt to escape Herod. Finally back to Nazareth to live, though every year they made yet another pilgrimage to Jerusalem. So many journeys that would teach them a whole new way of life and their dependency on others for welcome and hospitality.

Reflection

Set aside time during the next four weeks of Advent for pilgrimage. You don't have to travel far. You can take a mini pilgrimage around your city praying for the people you see along the way, praying over the police station, the city hall, the fire department, the hospital, buying lunch for a homeless person and listening to his/her story. Worshipping with another congregation in a different flavor.

A local pilgrimage might be hiking in silence along a trail with a group of friends, while pondering a passage of scripture and discussing it at a certain point along the way, processing it together, having time to journal on your own and hiking back out in silence. And processing the experience. Perhaps there are "holy places" near you you could visit, places where God has been worshiped for decades or centuries in and around your city/town.

A pilgrimage Includes daily times of reflection and prayer, praying the daily office together or a morning prayer time and an evening compline. We journey together to a new place. We live and work in community, sometimes with strangers. We practice silence, listening and bible study. We ponder questions together. We partake of the hospitality offered by others together, and we take time to rest and to just be with God. At the end of your pilgrimage take time to journal about your experience. What did you learn about yourself, about God and about the Advent and Christmas story?[19]

Oh, God, who brought your servants Abraham and Sarah
out of the land of the Chaldeans,
protecting them in their wanderings,
who guided the Hebrew people across the desert,
we ask that you watch over us, your servants,
as we walk in the love of your name.
Be for us our companion on the walk,
Our guide at the crossroads,
Our breath in our weariness,
Our protection in danger,
Our refuge on the way,
Our shade in the heat,
Our light in the darkness,
Our consolation in our discouragements,
And our strength in our intentions.
So that with your guidance we may arrive,
safe and sound,
at the end of the road
and, enriched with grace and virtue,
we may return safely to our homes
filled with joy.
In the name of Jesus Christ our Lord, Amen.[20]

November 21ˢᵗ — Guests of the World

Above all, love each other deeply, because love covers over a multitude of sins. Offer hospitality to one another without grumbling. Each of you should use whatever gift you have received to serve others, as faithful stewards of God's grace in its various forms. (1 Pet 4:8-10 NIV)

My husband Tom and I love to entertain and have, during our marriage offered hospitality many times to both friends and strangers. As we enjoy fun, food and fellowship together, I am very aware that, in some ways, all of us are guests, guests of God and of God's world, generously and lavishly experiencing the hospitality of a world that is itself a gift from God. I am aware of that as I pick raspberries and tomatoes in the early morning, enjoying the abundance of God's abundant provision. I am aware of it too as I gaze on the beauty around me at the mountains, the sea and the numerous plants in my garden. I love to breathe in the fragrance of God's presence.

Celtic saints, saw themselves as hospites mundi, or guests of the world, living lightly on this earth and not becoming attached to possessions or to one location. These followers of Christ saw all of life as a pilgrimage, a journey towards God. They believed that we live in perpetual exile, constantly seeking after Christ, and our outward journeys are to reflect our inner transformation. In exiling themselves from the comforts of home, pilgrims taught themselves to rely only on God.

The Celts had a saying for those setting out on pilgrimage: "Let your feet follow your heart until you find your place of resurrection." This was a spot where God's will for a pilgrim would be revealed and fulfilled. The place of resurrection need not be a famous holy site or a place far away. It could be a simple stone hut, a windswept island, or a secluded valley. The important thing was that each person needed to find their own site.

The welcoming of friends and strangers is deeply embedded in and referenced by Jesus as one of the signs of a true disciple as we see in Mathew 25:31-46, the story of separating the sheep from the goats. Celtic Christians embraced this spiritual discipline with enthusiasm. Stories abound in the Celtic tradition of hospitality shown not just to people but to animals as well. They were aware that sometimes in so doing, they might offer hospitality to angels unawares. Often this hospitality was given at extreme cost to the giver.

Recognizing ourselves as guests and pilgrims affects how we view everything that happens to us. Pilgrims and those who travel frequently do not presume anything. They travel lightly with few possessions, totally dependent on those they meet and the country they pass through. They learn to be grateful for comforts that those who never leave home take for granted. For a guest, each meal, especially a home cooked meal, is a gift of love from the host. Each bed provided for us to sleep in is a generous act of sharing and caring. Every journey accomplished safely is a provision of a caring God. Everything now becomes a gift of God.

According to Christine Pohl in her inspirational book *Making Room*, the tradition of hospitality was once an important part of all Christian communities and revolved around the welcoming of strangers into one's home. "For most of the history of the church, hospitality was understood to encompass physical, social, and spiritual dimensions of human existence and relationships. It meant response to the physical needs of strangers for food, shelter and protection, but also a recognition of their worth and common humanity. In almost every case, hospitality involved sharing meals: historically table fellowship was an important way of recognizing the equal value and dignity of persons."[21]

Mary too must have been very aware of her status as a guest of the world. First she was a guest of Elizabeth to whom I think she fled for safety after finding out she was pregnant, then to Joseph's family who may or may not have welcomed her in Bethlehem and finally to Egypt where she was welcomed as a refugee.

As you go about your work today, think of yourself as a guest of the world and prepare yourself for the amazing gifts of hospitality God wants to lavish on you – gifts of friendship, and food. Gifts of fellowship and love and caring, gifts of animals who pet and love you.

Reflection

Take a moment to pause and look around you. What do you notice that speaks of the generosity and hospitality of God? At home your attention may be caught by the dining room table, around which family and guests gather to eat and celebrate. Or photos and the gifts of friends and strangers to whom you have offered hospitality. Or maybe you are in the garden where even the wild brambles, and thistles – all the weeds you so diligently work to get rid of – are gifts from God and can produce the most delicious and nutritious food we can eat.

Sit in silent prayer to remind ourselves of the incredible hospitality of God who invites us, together with all creation, into the divine presence and into the eternal family.

God in this world of beauty,
We are your guests,
Receivers of your generous hospitality.
Beauty unimaginable surrounds us.
Abundance overflowing provides for us.
Joy indescribable strengthens us.
God in this world of brokenness
We are your hosts,
Called to give freely
Of your enduring love.
All we share
Is a thank offering to you.
Gratitude for your provision
Fills us.
Praise for your redemption,
Rises before us like incense.
Thankfulness for your love
Embraces us.
Receivers and givers,
Guests and hosts,
We are blessed,
By the wonder of your presence.

November 22nd — Radical Hospitality of Brigid

Keep on loving one another as brothers and sisters. Do not forget to show hospitality to strangers, for by so doing some people have shown hospitality to angels without knowing it. Continue to remember those in prison as if you were together with them in prison, and those who are mistreated as if you yourselves were suffering. (Hebrews 13: 1-3 NIV)

St. Brigid, is the patroness saint (or 'mother saint') of Ireland, and one of its three national saints along with Patrick and Columba. Brigid, who presided over the monastery at Kildare, was particularly known for her generous hospitality. Like other Celtic Christians her life was committed to sharing the love of Christ, often through practicing radical hospitality. She very much believed that offering hospitality was like receiving Christ into their midst and fulfilling the law of love.

Brigid was thought to be the child of an Irish noble and a slave woman. Unfortunately her life is shrouded in mystery and legend and often confused with the Celtic goddess Brigid a deity of wisdom, poetry, fire and hearth. Even her feast day, February 1st, coincides with the ancient festival Imbolc, when we celebrate the end of winter and the beginning of spring.

From an early age she showed a generous, hospitable and compassionate response to the poor and those in need which often made others uncomfortable. One story from her childhood I love tells of how her father became exasperated with her continually giving his possessions away to beggars and those in need so he decided to sell her to a king as a slave. When her father went to negotiate with the king, he made the mistake of leaving Brigid outside in his chariot with his sword which he had unbuckled and left behind as a sign of respect. A leper walked by asking for help and she gave him her father's sword, which as you can imagine made him extremely angry. The king watching the argument asked Brigid why she stole her father's property and gave it away. She reputedly responded "If I had the power I would steal all your wealth and give it to Christ's brothers and sisters." The king turned to Brigid's father and very diplomatically told him "I am afraid your daughter is too good for me, I could never win her obedience." So Brigid was saved from slavery and continued in her father's household until she took holy orders.

Brigid's generosity and hospitality to those in need continued throughout her life. She eventually became the Abbess at Kildare, the largest monastery in Ireland. At Kildare, from which she travelled around Ireland establishing other religious communities, it is said that she often made butter for visitors. Tradition has it that when churning the butter she would make thirteen portions – twelve in honour of the apostles and an extra one in honour of Christ which was reserved for guests and the poor. One of the things I love about Brigid is this strong emphasis on hospitality. Some of the beautiful Celtic hospitality blessings and runes we still know are attributed to her.

As I read this story I imagine Brigid welcoming Mary, Joseph and the unborn Jesus into her home when they arrived in Bethlehem. I imagine her feeding them, making them comfortable and giving them a bed to sleep in. Her welcome would have been generous and ongoing for as long as they were in need.

Reflection

Brigit reminds us that the hospitality of God is a welcoming of Christ into our midst. Reflect on the times that you have offered hospitality to friends and strangers. Where have you been aware of Christ in your midst at those times? Today many people are afraid to welcome strangers or the poor. Imagine ways you would be comfortable welcoming a stranger. Perhaps you could start by preparing a simple meal to take to a street person and say a prayer of blessing. How about inviting someone from church or your neighborhood who lives alone to dinner? There are often strangers in our midst who we see each week. What might be helpful to break down some of your barriers to entertaining strangers?

We saw a stranger yesterday,
we put food in the eating place,
Drink in the drinking place,
music in the listening place,
And with the sacred name of the triune God
He blessed us and our house,
our cattle and our dear ones.
As the lark says in her song:
Often, often, often goes the Christ
in the stranger's guise.[22]

November 23rd — Enjoying God's Wild Hospitality

Taste and see that the Lord is good;
blessed is the one who takes refuge in him.
Fear the Lord, you his holy people,
for those who fear him lack nothing. (Psalm 34:8,9 NIV)

There are two seasons of the year that invite us to radical hospitality - summer and Advent and much of this hospitality revolves around produce from our garden. Lush tomato salads in the summer, chocolate zucchini bread that I freeze and give as Christmas gifts during Advent. It always makes me very aware of the wonderful gifts of hospitality God constantly lavishes on us.

Several years ago, I spoke at a seminary class about spirituality and gardening at which a student asked "Didn't God curse the creation after the fall?", implying that it no longer reflected the glory of God and that we no longer needed to respect and look after it.

I was stunned. I am a strong believer in the goodness of all God's creation. I am always struck by God's amazing care for it in the face of human disobedience. Yes, the ground was cursed (Gen 3:17-19), but it was not God who cursed it, it was the consequence of Adam's sin. The natural created world, that God saw and proclaimed "It is very good" was somehow affected by human disobedience. Brambles and weeds grew. Human toil to produce food and care for creation increased. Nowhere however is there any implication that we are absolved from our responsibility to care for creation.

That summer I contemplated the thorns, the thistles, and the weeds that we all think of as part of the consequences of human disobedience. Some of them produce the most delicious and nutritious food we can eat. Take the humble dandelion for instance. Its leaves are often used in salads. Its root for medicinal tea and its flowers in jams and jelly. It helps break up the soil and draws nutrients up from deep within the soil. It is an amazing and valuable plant.

Then there is the blackberry which grows wild prolifically throughout the Pacific NW. It may be an invasive pest, and I know it chokes out many smaller native plants, including the native blackberry, but its fruit blesses us with delicious pies and jams, and birds butterflies and bees love them too. Every year in August Tom and I used to travel to Mayne Island, Canada with our Canadian friends Tom and Kim Balke, for a few days holiday. One of the delights of our trip was picking blackberries and wild apples to make blackberry apple crumble.

Snails are another pest that can be a delicacy for many. Ironically some people love escargot and spend big bucks to buy them and then complain about the snails that destroy their gardens. And in many Asian countries, tarantulas, crickets and ants are all considered delicacies.

Indigenous peoples are all very well aware of the wild hospitality of God and many other foragers have joined them in enjoying the rich harvest that the earth provides. Here in the Pacific NW salmonberries, native blackberries, huckleberries and elderberries are but a few of these delights. Then there are the mushrooms – chanterelles are our favorites but I love it when friends bring us morels, lion's mane and other delectable edible fungi straight from the forest.

Celtic Christians too were very aware of the wild hospitality offered by God's good creation. They fished and foraged and relied on the wild produce that flourished in the places in which they lived. They saw its goodness, recognized God's generous hospitality that it represented and rejoiced in the glory of God shining through it.

One delightful story tells of Columba visiting the graveyard on Iona and seeing an old woman cutting nettles. I am waiting for my cow to bear a calf she told him and until then I live on nettle soup. Columba decided that if she could do it so would he and ordered the monk who prepared his food to give him only nettle soup in future. The monk was afraid that this meagre diet would kill the abbot and so secretly added milk through a hollowed out stick to the soup. Columba thrived and the other monks wanted to share his strange diet. The poor monk in the kitchen ended up using all the milk at the monastery to make a huge cauldron of nettle soup and finally had to confess his trick to Columba. "It's God's spoke against me" he said "It was my pride that made me tell others. I deserve to be tricked." From then onwards he ordered a proper nutritious diet for all the monks.[23] Ironically nettle soup does have a high nutritional value, including calcium, magnesium, iron, and vitamins A and B. It is possible that it was the nettles as much as the milk that was good for Columba.

It seems to me that part of the curse we suffer from is our inability to recognize the abundance and hospitality of God in the garden that is our earth home. God is a generous God who invites us to a banquet feast, not just in the eternal world to come but here in this world too. Often all we need to do is reach out and recognize the gift and accept God's amazing hospitality.

Reflection

Take a walk around your garden or the closest nature reserve to your home. What "pests" do you see that really are part of the wild hospitality and abundance of God? Read through the poem below, attributed to Columba of Iona, which speaks of the love of creation and its hospitable gifts to us that is so much at the heart of Celtic spirituality.

Delightful it is to stand on the peak of a rock,
in the bosom of the isle, gazing on the face of the sea.
I hear the heaving waves chanting a tune to God in heaven; I see their glittering surf.
I see the golden beaches, their sands sparkling;
I hear the joyous shrieks of the swooping gulls.
I hear the waves breaking, crashing on the rocks, like thunder in heaven.
I see the mighty whales.
Contrition fills my heart as I hear the sea;
it chants my sins, sins too numerous to confess.
Let me bless almighty God, whose power extends over the sea and land,
whose angels watch over all.
Let me study sacred books to calm my soul;
I pray for peace, kneeling at heaven's gates.
Let me do my daily work, gathering seaweed, catching fish, giving food to the poor.
Let me say my daily prayers, sometimes chanting, sometimes quiet,
always thanking God.
Delightful it is to live on a peaceful isle, in a quiet cell, serving the King of kings.[24]

November 24th — Creation Hospitality with St. Kevin

The Word gave life to everything that was created,
and his life brought light to everyone.
The light shines in the darkness,
and the darkness can never extinguish it. (John 1:4,5 NLT)

There is within Celtic Christianity a deep appreciation of the natural world that grew out of the belief that all creation was birthed not out of a void of nothingness but out of the substance of God. All of creation is an expression of God and is filled with God's essence.

In *Christ of the Celts,* J. Philip Newell explains: "The great Irish teacher John Scotus Eriugena taught that God speaks to us through two books. One is the little book, he says, the book of scripture, physically little. The other is the big book, the book of creation, vast as the universe….Eriugena invites us to listen to the two books in stereo, to listen to the strains of the human heart in scripture and to discern within them the sound of God and to listen to the murmurings and thunders of creation and to know within them the music of God's Being. To listen to the one without the other is to only half listen. To listen to scripture without creation is to lose the cosmic vastness of the song. To listen to creation without scripture is to lose the personal intimacy of the voice… In the Celtic world, both texts are read in the company of Christ."[25]

This view of the earth is so important. How we view God's creation reflects our attitude towards it and towards God. If we believe this world is just a place to build our houses, drive our cars and dig for oil we will have a very utilitarian attitude towards it, with little respect or concern for its preservation. If we believe that it was created from the substance of God and reflects the glory of God, we see it as sacred, a beautiful tribute to the God who created it and loves it. It is to be reverenced (not worshipped) cared for and protected.

No Celtic saint more aptly portrays this connectedness of all creation than St. Kevin of Glendalough who was born in Ireland in the sixth century. He studied with three monks but very much wanted to be a hermit and one day ran away into the Wicklow mountains and came to the valley of Glendalough where eventually he established a monastery. His deepest call however was to live apart in the company of wild creatures, offering prayer and sacrifice to the living God. He prayed deeply and sometimes standing in the icy waters of a nearby lake with his arms outstretched. Sometimes he would sit in his hut with his arms outstretched through the window towards heaven. A blackbird, thinking his arm was a branch landed in his open palm and began to make a nest. When Kevin saw what the bird was doing he did not move but kept his arm in the same position while it laid its eggs and they hatched and were ready to fly away. He endured the pain because of his great love for the bird and for God.

Surely this intimacy of God with creation is nowhere more profoundly manifested than in the incarnation of Christ. That God honours the natural world by becoming part of it in the birth of Jesus is incredible. The incarnation speaks loudly of what God thinks of the natural world. God not only embraces and upholds it but cares passionately to the point of sanctifying it with the divine presence.

What difference would it make if we viewed everything as a translucent curtain through which the glory and wisdom of God shines? What difference would it make if we recognized the stunning revelation of God's concern for all of creation, not just humankind in the birth of Jesus. As John 3:16 says "God so loved the world he gave his only son" - not God so loved persons, but so God loved the world.

Reflection

How could you welcome creation during Advent? It might be with regular walks in your neighbourhood, by placing birdseed wreaths out for your feathered friends, or by standing outside to pray for a few minutes each day.
Grab your journal or a sheet of blank paper, a coloured crayon or pencil and a pen and head out into your closest green space, even if it is raining. Look around. What immediately catches your attention? Perhaps it is a rock of a certain shape, or a leaf of a special colour. It might even be a weed that you want to pull out! In what ways does the glory of God shine through it? Take a few moments to pay attention to the object and reflect on it in your journal. What aspect of God does it enhance for you? In what ways is God using it to nudge you in the right direction? As you complete this exercise consider how else you could welcome creation into your life this Advent season.

It were as easy for Jesu
To renew the withered tree
As to wither the new
Were it his will to do so.
Jesu! Jesu! Jesus!
Jesu! Meet it were to praise Him.
There is no plant in the ground
But is full of His virtue,

There is no form in the strand
But is full of His blessing.
Jesu! Jesu! Jesu!
Jesu! Meet it were to praise Him.
There is no life in the sea,
There is no creature in the river,
There is naught in the firmament,
But proclaims his goodness.
Jesu! Jesu! Jesu!
Jesu! Meet it were to praise Him.
There is no bird on the wing,
There is no star in the sky,
There is nothing beneath the sun,
But proclaims His goodness.
Jesu! Jesu! Jesu!
Jesu! Meet it were to praise Him.[26]

November 25th— Guests of St. Killian

From generation to generation,
*   God's lovingkindness endures*
*   for those who revere Him.*
God's arm has accomplished mighty deeds.
*   The proud in mind and heart,*
*   God has sent away in disarray.*
The rulers from their high positions of power,
*   God has brought down low.*
And those who were humble and lowly,
*   God has elevated with dignity.*
The hungry—God has filled with fine food.
*   The rich—God has dismissed with nothing in their hands.*
To Israel, God's servant,
*   God has given help,*
As promised to our ancestors,
*   remembering Abraham and his descendants in mercy forever.*
(Luke 2:51-55 The Voice)

To celebrate our 25th wedding anniversary Tom and I spent a couple of weeks in Britain visiting Iona, and spending time with friends. We then embarked on a wonderful river cruise up the Rhine and down the Danube from Amsterdam to Budapest. We then took the train to Prague and spent several days experiencing that wonderful city. This trip was a very special blessing for us as we have never before taken this much time just to celebrate friends, enjoy life and inhale the beauty of God's world. As the program director on board our ship said our cruise could have been featured on the brochures. The weather was almost perfect the whole way and we left with many incredible impressions and new friends.

So many provided hospitality for us along the way that we, like Celtic Christians before us, felt like guests of the world. As I reflected on our experiences I was most aware of those who have gone before us and made possible all that we did. I felt that they too were our hosts as we travelled and we were guests of their welcoming presence. We so rarely acknowledge them and yet their lives and sacrifices gave all of us the luxuries we so take for granted – luxuries of clean waterways, electricity, toilets, running water, good and abundant food.

I think of the Celtic monks who we first encountered in Iona off the west coast of Scotland. These men and women who kept the spark of faith alive throughout the Dark Ages. In Würzburg, Germany we met them again when we were introduced to Killian and his companions Kolonat and Totnan who re-evangelized this part of central Europe, possibly having travelled from Iona. They were martyred around 689 but their lives still impact this part of the world. The day after our visit was St. Killian's feast day, still celebrated in Würzburg with joy. For many Germans, Killian is a family name, including our good friend Hans Greulich whom we met with in Passau. His grandfather is called Killian. Their faith was like a light shining in the chaotic days of Europe during the Dark Ages.

As we sailed past, and then visited some of the castles along the Rhine river I thought too of those who endured much hardship throughout the centuries to give us the freedoms we have today. They cultivated crops in harsh environments, endured epidemics and fought their foes. They lived in ways that we would never endure today. I thought too of those who lost their lives in wars. So many of the towns we stopped at were 90% destroyed during WW II. Reduced to piles of rubble like we see now in Ukraine and Gaza. Amazingly, many of them have been rebuilt not in modern style but as they were before.

I think too of those who designed the breathtaking cathedrals we visited, crafted the mighty organ we listened to in Passau Germany and composed the music we relished in Vienna Austria. Their creativity was a gift of hospitality to us.

Finally, I remember my parents whose frugality provided us with the resources that we were able to spend on that trip. They too are our hosts. I particularly felt my mother's welcoming presence beside me as we travelled. I was her guest on this trip just as much as I was when I stayed in her house in Australia.

I wonder as I look back on this journey how aware Mary was of those who went before her as she walked through her pregnancy. All those ancestors whose names are recorded in the gospel of Matthew. The Old Testament stories of the exodus from Egypt, the entry into the promised land and the promises of a Messiah who would bring freedom and justice to their broken society that she grew up with. Did she think of them and thank them, recognizing the hospitality of their actions that led to her now carrying the Christ child?

Reflection

We are blessed people who rarely stop to acknowledge our blessings. Stop and reflect today on those who have gone before you, gifting you through their labours with life, and freedom and comfort. If possible get out photos of people and places you want to thank God for. Read through the scripture above which is an excerpt from the Magnificat as you reflect on the questions below.

- Remember your parents and your ancestors and the struggles they went through to make your comfortable lifestyle possible. Remind yourself of those in your lineage who carried the spark of faith. Offer a prayer of thanksgiving to God for them.
- Remember those who pioneered your country or the area in which you live. Thank them for their sacrifices and the ways their lives have provided hospitality for you. Offer a prayer of thanks to God.
- Remember those who sacrificed their lives in wars to give you freedom. Thank them for the gift of life which you enjoy because of their sacrifice.

God you surround us with a cloud,
Faithful hosts who have gone before.
Those who loved when we would have hated.
Those who healed when we would have hurt.
Those who spoke out when we would have remained silent.
May we walk in their footsteps.
Learn courage from their sacrifice.
Gain strength from their faithfulness.
We are their guests,
Welcomed by their lives and their sacrifices,
And we give thanks for their bountiful gifts.

November 26th — Hosting the World with St. Melangell

"Look! God's dwelling is here with humankind. He will dwell with them, and they will be his peoples. God himself will be with them as their God. He will wipe away every tear from their eyes. Death will be no more. There will be no mourning, crying, or pain anymore, for the former things have passed away." (Revelation 21:3,4 CEB)

Have you ever considered how incredibly hospitable our Creator is? Today I sit in awe as I consider the amazing story of creation and the generous hospitality our Maker displays. God created a world in which all forms of life, from the smallest microbe to the tallest tree, were meant to live in hospitable harmony together, giving and sharing with each other as God intended. Then God invited humanity to be both the hosts and guests of that world, encouraging all of us to look after this glorious creation in a way that would make everything from the smallest microbe to the tallest tree feel welcomed and comfortable.

It is easy for us to see God as our host, but God as our guest is another matter. In his inspirational book *A New Heaven and A New Earth* Richard Middleton suggests that humans were supposed to transform the whole earth into a fitting place, a hospitable place, not just for all creatures, but also for God to dwell. Can you imagine it? God longs for a beautiful place where all creation flourishes and enjoys abundant provision, a place in which God too feels welcomed and comfortable, able to walk once more in a hospitable relationship with humankind.

It seems to me that the Celtic saints were very aware of this upside down relationship. When they invited strangers and animals into their homes and monasteries they did so with the expectation that they could be entertaining angels or Christ as a guest unawares.

St. Melangell whose story has permeated the valley of the Bergwyns in Wales since the seventh century is a great example of this. According to the *Historia*, Melangell was a princess of Ireland who fled an arranged marriage looking for a place to practice prayer and solitude. She lived in the wilderness of valley of the Bergwyn Mountains for fifteen years before prince Brochwell, hunting near Pennant (now Pennant Melangell) with his dogs, chased a hare that led him to Melangell devoutly praying, with the hare lying safe under the hem of her dress. The prince urged the dogs on, but they retreated and fled from Melangell and the hare.

After hearing Melangell's story, Brochwel donated the land to her, granting perpetual asylum to both the people and animals of the area. Melangell founded and became abbess of a community of nuns. The valley became known as a holy place of prayer where anyone in danger or distress could find a safe haven. The hares and wild animals also found sanctuary there and behaved towards Melangell as if they were tamed. Miracles were attributed to them. Even today the little church in the valley is a place of prayer, and provides refuge for wandering souls.

When we host people or animals in our homes for meals or extend a welcome of any kind to another person as Melangell did, we should expect to meet Jesus in that person or that creature.

In the birth of Jesus, God becomes a guest of our world once more. The unbelievable gift of Jesus was one of amazing hospitality towards all of us. Here in the birth of the son of God to an unwed mother, at the fringes of society we see the wonder of a God who comes as a guest to the vulnerable and the outcast, to the excluded and the disregarded, born in the middle of the natural world, where all the creatures of creation watch. Throughout Jesus' life, we continue to catch glimpses of what that world into which God wants to be invited could look like. We need to live in the hopeful imagination of such a world and the confident anticipation of its coming.

Reflection

Each of us has the opportunity to transform our own little space as a place of welcome for God. In the garden it might mean doing away with pesticides and harsh chemicals, but in our lives it means doing away with hatred and discrimination and indifference to other humans and to all of creation.

Sit for a few moments and consider what kind of world you think God wants to be invited into. Write a description or draw a picture in your journal. Prayerfully consider what you might do to make your own little space a more hospitable place for God to dwell.

It was billions of years in the making,
This delightful banquet
We call our earthly home.
A banquet of rivers and lakes,
Of rain and sparkling sunshine,
Of rich earth and wondrous flowers.
A feast of magnificent trees and dancing birds,
Of majestic animals and whistling winds,
Of dry and wet seasons, cold and hot climates,
God's wild hospitality where we are welcomed as guests,
With abundant and generous provision for all life.
Imagine this world when people are justly treated,
Free from the burden of pollution.
And all creation flourishes,
And all people rejoice in fruitful and fulfilling labour.
Imagine if all children carried the hope
Of a vibrant and healthy future,
In a world restored, renewed and made whole.
Imagine a world in which God once more feels welcomed,
And lives in harmony with all created life.
Our host but also our guest.

Week 3 —

Reaching For Hope

November 27th — Pelagius' Unfamiliar Path toward Hope

Heaven is declaring God's glory;
the sky is proclaiming his handiwork.
One day gushes the news to the next,
and one night informs another what needs to be known.
Of course, there's no speech, no words—
their voices can't be heard—
but their sound[a] extends throughout the world;
their words reach the ends of the earth. (Psalm 19: 1-4 CEB)

One of the things I love about the Celtic tradition is the new perspectives it brings to my view of faith and of the world. Take the Celtic monk and theologian Pelagius for example. Born in Wales, he was the first writer and teacher of significance in Celtic Britain, but was dismissed by Augustine of Hippo as a heretic and excommunicated from the church. To the Celts, he was a breath of fresh air and still brings that freshness and hope to many of us who follow this tradition today.

In *Sacred Earth, Sacred Soul,* John Philip Newell points out that for 1500 years, Pelagius' name has been condemned for its supposed teaching that humanity is capable of saving itself without the aid of divine grace. However, Newell goes on to explain that this is not really what Pelagius taught. He emphasized that what is deepest within us is the image of God and when we look into the face of a newborn, we are looking into the face of God freshly born among us. "Pelagius was not speaking merely of the newborn child. He was speaking also of what is deepest in every human being. He was enunciating the dignity of our human nature, as he put it, not the defilement of our nature. He was emphasizing our sacredness over our sinfulness.... He was teaching that what is deepest in us is of God, not opposed to God. This is what we can see clearly in the face of a newborn child."[27] Sin has buried the beauty of God's image but not erased it. The gospel is given to uncover the hidden wealth of God that is plated in the depths of our human nature.[28] What a revolutionary and refreshing statement. There is a God-placed deep yearning within all of us. Jesus came not to save us from our sinful nature but to guide that yearning and uncover the image of God hidden deep within each of us.

Pelagius also believed in the sacredness of nature. God's spirit is in all living things "and if we look with God's eyes, nothing on the earth is ugly." This belief led him to call on the Roman Empire to treat the earth and its resources with reverence and see that it was equitably shared.[29]

Pelagius saw God and God's kingdom through the lenses of a Celt who loved God's world and knew deep in their soul that God's Spirit, the *ruah*, the very breath of God was blown into *all* of creation. This view of God's creation as good and sacred and holy was dramatically different than the Roman view of life in which all of humanity and creation are depraved.[30] Though Pelagius was excommunicated, his ideas obviously lived on in the Celtic love of nature and reverence for the poor and those in need.

Jewish wisdom as revealed in the Pentateuch, which Mary and Joseph grew up with, is rooted in this same kind of reverence for all of life. In The Eco Bible Volume One, Rabbi David Rosen explains the ecological impact of the Bible's opening verse: "If you believe that this world is the creation of a Divine Power, therefore creation itself manifests the Divine Presence, as it says in Psalms, "The heavens declare the glory of God and the firmament declares the work of His hands." If you are a Divinely sensitive person, whether you want to define that as religious or spiritual, then the wellbeing, the health of the environment, and of creation, is a religious imperative." [31]

Can you imagine what a radical difference it would make to how we treat our fellow human beings and God's good earth if we had this attitude? To see all of creation as sacred and to recognize the spark of divinity within every human being means that we treat everything and everyone with reverence and respect. We care for others as we do ourselves, we welcome friend and stranger and we love God's creation with the same concern.

Reflection

The human face is an incredible artistic achievement and no two faces are the same. Each face, each person is a unique and beautiful creation of the interweaving of human and Godly presence. Yet so often when we meet people we do not look them in the eye. We do not examine their faces for the presence of God. We are often more concerned with telling others about our interests than in hearing about what they think. How do you look at the people you meet? Who are the people you find it difficult to look at? Do you gaze at them looking for the image of God hidden within them or do your eyes not focus on them at all?

Look in the mirror at your own reflection. Ask yourself 'What of the image of God is present in me?' As you do so, remind yourself that you are God's beloved child.

Now, take time today to fully engage the people you meet, those you enjoy and those you find difficult to relate to and recognize the belovedness of God within them. Focus on their faces. Listen to what they say and ask yourself "What of the image of God is present in this person?" Journal about what you learn.

I should like a great lake of finest ale,
for the King of Kings
I should like a table of the choicest food,
for the family of heaven.
Let the ale be made from the fruits of faith,
and the food be forgiving love.
I should welcome the poor to my feast,
for they are God's children.
I should welcome the sick to my feast,
for they are God's joy.
Let the poor sit with Jesus at the highest place,
and the sick dance with the angels.
God bless the poor,
God bless the sick,
and bless our human race.
God bless our food,

God bless our drink,
all homes, O God, embrace.[32]

November 28th — Carmina Gadelica
Awakening Hope

Lord, you have done so many things!
You made them all so wisely!
The earth is full of your creations!
Let the Lord's glory last forever!
Let the Lord rejoice in all he has made! (Psalm 104: 24,31 CEB)

In the Celtic world it was poetry, songs, prayers and blessings passed down by oral tradition, that most powerfully expressed the wisdom of the human soul. These poems and blessings were used throughout life: from birth to death, from dawn to dusk, from season to season. They encompassed every mundane act of life from lighting the fire in the morning to banking it at night, from making the bed, to milking the cow. There are prayers for going on a journey, for greeting friends and welcoming strangers. Even the monastic rule followed by the Irish monks was written in poetic form. Some of the prayers are thought to date back to Columba on Iona.

Unlike so many of our prayers today, the Celtic prayers almost never ask God for anything directly. Instead they recognize that God is present and active all around us and they call for those blessings to be made real in our own lives.

Celtic prayers, poems and the rituals that were practiced with them would have been lost to us except for the work of Alexander Carmichael, an excise man, born of the island of Lismore in the Inner Hebrides. He spent all of his life in the islands, travelling in the latter part of the 19th century, collecting a rich array of these prayers, poems and the rituals and stories that accompanied them. He transcribed them from Gaelic to English and in 1900 began publishing them under the title *Carmina Gadelica (The Song of the Gaels.)*[33]

At the same time, Douglas Hyde, who belonged to the Society for the Preservation of the Irish Language, published more than a hundred pieces of Irish verse under the pen name *An Craoibhín Aoibhinn.* He was an Irish academic, linguist, scholar of the Irish language, politician, and diplomat who in later life served as the first President of Ireland from June 1938 to June 1945.[34]

It was these prayers that first attracted me to the Celtic tradition. They are a source of hope and joy for me. Through them, I discovered the beauty and the joy of translating my own thoughts and emotions into written prayers and poems. I often start with one of the ancient prayers and then translate it into my own impressions and ideas. The writing of such prayers and poems helps me to slow down, breathe deeply and take notice of the voice of God bubbling up from deep within me. As well as that, reading them aloud resonates deep within my body and seems to lodge in my soul. Poetry is a powerful force of hope that can transform not only the poet's life but also the lives of others who read it and allow it to resonate in their hearts.

There are several reasons why poetry is so good at expressing our emotions. First, emotional undertones are hard to put into words. The metaphor and imagery that takes shape in a poem often helps us give voice to them. Poetic rhythms tap into powerful nonverbal responses, in much the same way that music does. Even the abstract nature of poetry is a powerful tool that makes it easier to take a closer look at painful experiences which can be threatening to us if we try to approach them in a direct manner.

Poetry is not just about words. Sometimes we begin with a word. At other times it is a thought or an image that resonates in our minds. It calls to us, perhaps out of the depths of our pain, or through flashes of intense joy or awe inspiring wonder. The image grows and takes shape emerging into words that burst out of our mouths. We recite them aloud, sensing the vibrations not just in our ears but also in our hearts and minds. They pluck at our heartstrings and slowly we craft them into a cascade of verses that brings healing and refreshment in mind, soul and body.

The Bible is full of poetic images like this that pull at our heartstrings and beckon us to listen to the voice of God, healing and cleansing our spirits on the way. Sometimes we feel that these ancient books cannot fully express what bubbles up within us. Spoken prayers and words of adoration and praise don't seem to do it either. We need poetic language from our own hearts to enable us to interpret the pain and the joy of life in our own unique and expressive way.

In the Old Testament, Isaiah and the Psalms are my two favourite poetic books and I suspect it was the words and ideas from these books that overflowed from within Mary and Zechariah's hearts to burst forth in their own poetic utterances. And now their poetic words continue to inspire us each Advent as we allow them to sink into our hearts and resonate in our souls.

Reflection

Several years ago I started a a special journal in which to record prayers and poems I write. I love returning to this at the end of the year to remind myself of what stirred my passions during the year. Similar to the monks who did the art and calligraphy for the Book of Kells, we absorb what we take time to carefully reflect on. What kinds of poems and prayers resonate with you? Perhaps you too would like to create a special journal to record your prayers and poems and the insights they give you into life and the world around you.

Where in your life, would you like to see hope re-awakened? Read the ancient Celtic poem below aloud and allow it to resonate within you. Is there a particular stanza that speaks to your heart and brings you hope? Read it through again and then use it as a template for writing your own prayer of worship and protection.

God to enfold me,
God to surround me,
God in my speaking,
God in my thinking.

God in my sleeping,
God in my waking,
God in my watching,
God in my hoping.

God in my life,
God in my lips,
God in my hands,
God in my heart.[35]

November 29th — Welcoming Guides like St. Cuthbert

Faith is the reality of what we hope for, the proof of what we don't see. The elders in the past were approved because they showed faith.
(Hebrews 11:1,2 CEB)

Several years ago Tom and I had the privilege of visiting St. Catherine's monastery in the Sinai desert. This is one of the oldest working monasteries in existence, and monastic life in the area dates back to the 4th century. Evidently at one point there were something like 3,000 hermits living in the hills around the site.

However the history of St. Catherine's monastery goes much further back than that. Tradition has it that St. Catherine's monastery sits at the base of Mt Sinai. Many believe that is also the site for Moses's encounter with God in the midst of the burning bush.

I wonder what it must have been like for the Israelites to live out in the desert. Fortunately God did not send them out without a well seasoned guide. Moses spent many years in the desert in his early life, and seems to have brought them back to the part of the desert that he was familiar with. Maybe even to the home that he lived in for all those years, the place where he raised his family, and knew how to live without allowing the desert to consume him.

Moses knew how to find water, how to track animals and how to provide shelter. And God also provided a cloud to guide them through the day and a pillar of fire to light the night. Talk about overkill, but a people who were not used to desert life probably needed a lot of help in finding their way. Without Moses their hope would have turned to despair.

The Celtic Christians were deeply influenced by the desert fathers and mothers maybe by some of those same monks who lived as hermits around St. Catherine's monastery. They carried the monastic tradition surrounded by hermits with them into Gaul and then to Ireland, Scotland and Wales where monasticism contributed to the spread of Christianity. They didn't need to struggle with deserts but with cold wildness and harsh weather. They often settled in hard to reach places usually starting as hermits who cleared a piece of forest and built a hut. Others were attracted to them and more huts were built followed by a chapel. In some cases, thousands of people followed and large settlements developed.

The leaders often continued to long for the hermit's life however. Cuthbert of Lindisfarne for example was a gifted preacher and teacher known for his holy gentleness. He became an abbot and a bishop but would often retreat to Lindisfarne, a tidal island which is cut off from the mainland twice a day by the tides, for prayer and solitude. Even this was not isolated enough for him and he sought the more isolated island of Inner Farne which has neither water, food nor trees. Here he entered into even deeper prayer and listening, offering his life as a living prayer. Often he prayed at night standing in the sea with his arms extended, his body resembling a cross. According to legend, as he walked ashore after hours of prayer, two otters came and dried his feet with their fur. Even here Cuthbert could not escape the seekers who, drawn by his Christlike qualities, came seeking counsel and wisdom. His life guided many towards a passion for Christ.

God does not leave any of us alone without lots of well seasoned guides either. Our loving Creator knows that without the witness of those who have gone before we often lose hope and struggle with despair. It is reassuring to know that millions of followers of Christ have walked out into their own wildernesses led by God, and not only survived but thrived and grown in intimacy with God as a result of their experiences.

I wonder who Mary's guides were? Elizabeth seems to have been one. An older supportive woman who provided a safe haven during the early days of her pregnancy. Did she also look back to women like Deborah the prophetess who settled disputes for the Hebrews and Rahab the prostitute who kept the Israelite spies safe from the soldiers of Jericho? Or maybe she thought of her ancestresses Bathsheba who was so badly treated by King David - possibly raped, her husband murdered and then her first child dying at an early age, or Ruth the Moabite who became David's grandmother. So many strong women to guide and support her and give her hope for the future.

Reflection

What have been some of your wilderness experiences? Who are the guides that wandered in the desert ahead of you and helped establish a home for you? Who are the ones you can rely on to find water, food and shelter for you in desert times and places? Who are the ones that fill you with hope as you look at the journey ahead? Some of them may be friends and family members who inspire and support you. Others may be ancestors or still others Celtic saints like Patrick, Columba and Brigid or other saints like Julian of Norwich whose life and witness took on new significance during COVID as she lived during the 14th century in the midst of the bubonic plague. They have guided not just my life but all our lives in wilderness times. Make a list and consider getting in touch with them to thank them for their input into your life. Pray for them and take time to give thanks to God for them today.

May the lingering echo
Of God's beloved ones,
Who still walk beside and within us,
Touch our hearts.
May their stories
Of courage and perseverance,
In the face of adversity,
Guide and support us,
Lodging in the inner places of our being.
May they open space
For the Spirit to enter us afresh.
May the God of every generation
Inspire us with hope
For this and future generations,
And for the broken world
In which we live.

November 30th — A Perilous Journey in Ethiopia

The angel said, "Don't be afraid, Zechariah. Your prayers have been heard. Your wife Elizabeth will give birth to your son and you must name him John. He will be a joy and delight to you, and many people will rejoice at his birth, for he will be great in the Lord's eyes. (Luke 1:13-15 CEB)

Abuna Yemata Guh is a monolithic church located in the Hawzen woreda of the Tigray Region, Ethiopia. It is situated at a height of 2,580 metres (8,460ft) and has to be climbed on foot and in bare feet to reach. It is notable for its dome and beautiful wall paintings dating back to the 5th century.

Hmm, this doesn't sound like Celtic Christianity you might say and you are right. However, the Celtic Christians were deeply influenced by the desert fathers and mothers of Egypt and Syria. In fact on many of the high crosses of Ireland is a scene that depicts two hermits, St. Antony of Egypt and St. Paul of Thebes, meeting together in the Egyptian desert. These same desert fathers and mothers also impacted the Coptic and Ethiopian Orthodox Church.

Abuna Yemata Guh fascinates me. The perilous journey parishioners must take in order to worship in this ancient church is incredible and to me very reminiscent of the journeys that Celtic saints took to worship God. Despite the scary climb, the church is active with churchgoers climbing up the cliffs several times a week including mothers with their children on their back, pregnant women, babies and old people to attend services. Evidently young mothers bring their infants to be baptized here because they see it as being closer to heaven, more powerful and therefore closer to God than the churches on the plain below. Not surprisingly, there are well worn impressions in the sandstone where thousands of people have trod over the last almost 1500 years.

Fortunately the Abuna Yemata Guh church also has a local guide and guards at every step of the climb, making sure visitors know which foothold to take and which rock to climb. They also help out with the ropes.

Sharing about this church seems appropriate for us in the middle of our Celtic Advent journey. As I watched a video of women bringing their infants to be baptized when they were just 40 days old, I was struck by the dedication of these mothers to their children and the desire to see them receive the most powerful and Godly blessing possible for their lives.[36] They were filled with hope that this perilous journey would provide blessings for their offspring throughout their lives.

Imagine the perilous journeys that Mary and Joseph took, first when she was pregnant accompanying Joseph to Bethlehem. Then after Jesus' birth the even more perilous journey into Egypt. Mary and Joseph were even more dedicated to the wellbeing of their child who they believed would one day become the Messiah so long promised to the Jewish people. Their journeys were more dangerous and more disruptive of their lives than they ever imagined. They too were filled with hope, however, hope that this child conceived by the Holy Spirit would indeed, one day transform the world.

Abuna Yemata Guh, makes me ponder my own faith journey – now entering its 59th year. I was not prepared for the ways that this journey would totally upend and transform my life either. There were many points at which I considered turning aside, but the call of God on my life was so strong and so insistent, that I could not do that. I suspect Mary and Joseph moved with the same sense of calling and the worshippers at Abuna Yemata Guh seem to as well. I wonder how often those climbing to the church to worship, felt like turning back. Did they find hope and courage from the footsteps of those who had gone before? Did they find strength in the story of Mary and Joseph and especially from their long and perilous flight into Egypt which is at the heart of the Coptic church? There is so much that we can learn from ancient places and ancient traditions like this that hopefully draw us closer to the presence of God.

Reflection

Pull out a sheet of paper and some pens and draw a picture that depicts your own faith journey. What are some of the markers along the way in your journey? Were there points at which you were afraid because of how perilous it was? Mark these in red. Were there times you considered turning back? Mark these in blue. Spend time reflecting on what kept you moving forward when life got difficult. In what ways did these experiences change you and enrich your faith? You might like to journal about your understanding of how God has been walking with you, and how God connects various points of your journey.

Jesus friend, companion, lover of my soul,
The One who walks beside me
Wherever I might go.
The One who holds me close
When despair lurks at the door,
And comforts me,
When the way is rough
And I stumble over rocks
I did not see.
Walk with me now,
Through all the twists and turns of life,
When clouds obscure the way,
When what once seemed close,
Now looks so far away.
Walk with me
Down paths of light,
And trails of dark,
Hold me lest I fall.
Until I trust in you
And journey into the light
At the centre of your love.

December 1st — Finding Hope with St. Ciarán

Because of our God's deep compassion,
the dawn from heaven will break upon us,
to give light to those who are sitting in darkness
and in the shadow of death,
to guide us on the path of peace." (Luke 1:78,79 CEB)

Several years ago one of our summer interns walked into Seattle from our home, photographing images of despair on the way in and images of hope on the way back. Images of despair were easy, those of hope much harder to find. Bad news travels fast and is much louder than good. We must very intentionally hunt for the images of hope and good news. So where do I find the hope that helps me balance my concerns for the devastation of our world and horrors of war, starvation and abuse with my joy in beauty, goodness and hope?

To be honest I have not always been a hope filled person and sometimes I still wallow in despair. It is heartbreaking to see the ongoing violence in Ukraine, Gaza and Sudan. We seem further from the peaceful world of Christmas promise than ever. However, several tactics can turn my emotions around and encourage me to respond with hope rather than hopelessness.

First, I look for hope in the scriptures. Tom once asked me to write a prayer on hope for an evening gathering. Hope, I thought, what is there to be hopeful about? So I went looking for hope. I searched the Bible for the word hope, comparing three different versions. Some verses proclaimed where our hope lay – in the eternal God, in Christ our instructor, in God's call to be a covenant family and to seek God's eternal kingdom of love, peace, justice and compassion. Others described hope – never ending, ever present, never failing. By the time I finished my prayer I found that my own emotional state had changed completely. I regained my hope in God and God's eternal purposes.

Second, I reframe the question "Why does God allow bad things to happen?" Instead I ask "Where is God in the midst of this disaster?" Every time I hear about the risks that first responders put themselves at to fight wildfires, repair flood damage or search for people trapped after an earthquake I think "That is God at work". Knowing that strangers come from half a world away to help people in the midst of disasters is incredible. Seeing young people dedicate their lives to see our planet better cared for and people at the margins provided for, fills me with awe. These are signs of a God who cares and who has placed that caring ability deep within all of us.

Third, I express my gratitude for the good things I see around me. Every time I express gratitude to someone or for something, I feel my spirit lift. One of my Sunday practices is to remind myself of all that I am grateful for in the past week. Writing these down is often very hope giving and always brings a smile to my face.

Fourth, I look for signs of hope in the world around me and in the lives of those who have gone before. St. Ciarán of Ireland is one who gives me hope today. He is known as one of the twelve apostles of Ireland, a friend of both animals and people and founder of the great monastic city of Clonmacnoise, one of the largest, richest and most important monastic centers of learning in the entire Celtic church.[37] Unfortunately he died a year later at the age of 33, but the monastery continued to flourish and became a center of learning and devotion for all of Europe, a bright shining light in the dark ages. Tom and I had the privilege of visiting this beautiful site on the banks of the Shannon River. It still contains some of the most magnificent Celtic crosses and monastic ruins in Ireland and is visited by many pilgrims each year.

In spite of his short life Ciarán was well known for his love of learning and his great capacity for friendships. He had a broad network of soul friends scattered throughout the early Irish church, including Columcille of Iona (a fellow student), Finial of Clonard (his tutor), Enda of the Aran Islands (a mentor), Senan of Scattery Island (a colleague) and Kevin of Glendalough (a close friend). [38]

Even though Ciarán did not live to see the fulfillment of his dream, he trusted in the God of hope to begin this community and I am sure died trusting God and the hope that it would continue and flourish. What an incredible account of a life that gives us hope for the future.

Mary too, must have lived in hope, trusting in the God of hope, to fulfill all that she felt was promised to her in the birth of the child she carried. Her hope rested on the promises of the Hebrew people for a Messiah coming who would bring resurrection life to her people and in fact to all the people of the world.

Reflection

What gives you hope at this season of your life, not just for yourself and your family but for the whole planet? Hope often comes in the small and insignificant aspects of life - the colour of a flower, the smile of a child, the laughter of friends. Take a few moments to look around. Think of the little things in your family, your home, your neighbourhood that give you hope. Take some photos, make a list, give thanks to God. Now think of our planet. What gives you hope and encourages you to believe that God is not only in control but is slowly making all things new?

Lord Jesus Christ you wait for us,
To come and see you.
You wait to shine light where there is darkness,
To show love where there is hate,
To share peace where there is conflict,
To give hope where there is despair.
Lord Jesus Christ you wait for us,
To come and see you.
You wait for us to gather round your birth,
To shine your light,
To show your love,
To share your peace,
To give your hope to our suffering world.
Let us come in hope and expectation,
Remembering what has been fulfilled,
Preparing for what must yet be done.

Let us come,
To the One who waits to show us love.

December 2nd — Waiting in Hope with St. Hilda

We put our hope in the Lord.
He is our help and our shield.
Our heart rejoices in God
because we trust his holy name.
Lord, let your faithful love surround us
because we wait for you. (Psalm 33: 20-22 CEB)

We are living in challenging times. The threat of climate change, war and violence around the world, political divides that seem insurmountable have us all oscillating between despair and hope. In the midst of venting our strong feelings it is easy to lose our ability to listen to each other and so increase the conflict and the divide between us. Hope so easily gives way to despair and faith is replaced by doubt.

Transitions are always uncomfortable. Moving from the familiar through the unknown into something new that has never been seen before brings out all of our insecurities. It often creates turmoil, discord and unrest. Restoring our hope in God at times like this can, however, be a transforming experience.

Hilda of Whitby must have known a lot about the insecurity of maintaining hope in the midst of change and conflict. She organized several communities of faith in Northumbria and founded a double monastery in Whitby, which combined separate communities of monks and nuns, possibly even married couples, joined in one institution to share one church and other facilities. She not only encouraged learning at the monastery but also set up a rule of life that balanced prayer, asceticism, and the sharing of material goods. Her reputation as a talented abbess and much loved spiritual guide contributed to King Oswy's choice of Whitby as the place to hold a council in 664.

This synod took place in the context of a significant cultural and religious divide in England. At the time, there were two main Christian streams. The contrast between them was stark. The Roman tradition came with pomp and ceremony, brought to England by missionaries from Rome. It accentuated the doctrine of original sin and firmly subordinated the role of women. The Celtic tradition came with simplicity and generosity to the poor, brought by missionaries from Ireland and Scotland. Like the Eastern Orthodox tradition it celebrated the dignity of the divine spark in the heart of every man and woman and practiced priestly marriage. The different practices and beliefs of the Celtic tradition and the Roman Catholic Church created considerable disagreement and often heated arguments between them. This important meeting was called to decide questions in dispute between the two parties related to the dating of Easter, the nature of the monk's tonsure and other ecclesiastical matters. I suspect that the choice of Hilda, a female abbess as hostess for this event was controversial in itself.

Although Hilda was sympathetic to the Celtic church's expression of faith, she encouraged others to follow the pathway that would lead to unity and formation of one church. It must have been a very challenging and painful time for her. All of Lindisfarne's Irish monks and 30 of their English brothers were so distraught that they left for Ireland via Iona. The decade that ensued saw conflicts in church and state. Whitby under Hilda's leadership, seems to have been an anchor of calm amid a sea of storms. Through it all she showed common sense, informed by a concern that the church should be just in its dealings. She was not afraid to stand up for people who were being misrepresented, yet she took a stand in such a way that people on all sides acknowledged her spiritual authority. She bore no grudges and eschewed prejudices and judgmental words. She truly became a transcultural spiritual mother.[39]

The decision of the Synod of Whitby had far-reaching consequences for the church in England. It led to the gradual adoption of Roman practices and traditions, and the retreat of the Celtic church. If Hilda had known that in the twentieth century interest in the Celtic church would be revived, with the establishment of monastic orders like the Northumbria Community, the Community of Aidan and Hilda and the Iona community I wonder how she would have felt.

Mary and Joseph looked back over many hundreds of years of waiting and hoping by their people. I imagine that it had often been hard to keep this hope alive. The spark of life Mary carried in her body must have been an incredible hope-giving one, not just for Mary and Joseph, Elizabeth and Zechariah but for all who knew them and heard their stories.

Reflection

Who has given you hope when you felt hopeless? Who has provided light when you lived in darkness and felt the darkness was forever? Pause to bring to mind those who stood with you and gave you hope when life seemed to go in the wrong direction. Visualize them standing with you as you walk through Advent. Offer prayers of gratitude and thanksgiving for them.

Now think about those for whom you have brought hope. Who stands with you because you held their hands or helped heal their bodies when they were in need? Offer prayers of gratitude and thanksgiving for them.

Be Thou a smooth way before me,
Be Thou a guiding star above me,
Be Thou a keen eye behind me,
This day, this night, for ever.
I am weary, and forlorn,
Lead Thou me to the land of the angels;
Methinks it were time I went for a space
To the court of Christ, to the peace of heaven.
If only Thou, O God of life,
Be at peace with me, be my support,
Be to me as a star, be to me as a helm
From my lying down in peace to my rising anew.[40]

December 3rd — Hope in A Wounded Healer - St. Winefride

The mind of the wise makes their speech insightful
and enhances the teaching of their lips.
Pleasant words are flowing honey,
sweet to the taste and healing to the bones. (Prov. 16: 23,24 CEB)

I first met St. Winefride in Ellis Peters' wonderful mystery series starring the 12th century monk Cadfael. In the first story, the monastery at Shewsbury decides they need a patron saint and choose Welsh Winefride buried at Holywell in Wales. Cadfael and a deputation of monks from Shrewsbury are dispatched to Wales to recover her remains over the objections of the local lord and residents. Cadfael is Welsh and horrified at the thought of moving this holy saint's bones and through subterfuge manages to leave the bones in their original grave while giving the abbott the impression that they have been moved in the ornate box provided to Shewsbury where it was hoped that pilgrims would come to be healed by the saint. From Cadfael's perspective, Saint Winifred's magic doesn't need to be constrained by distance.

Obviously this is a fanciful story, but the legend of St. Winefride sounds just as fanciful. She was born to a wealthy family in Northern Wales in the 7th century. Evidently from an early age she felt a strong attachment to Christ and wanted to lead a holy life. Her family supported her so she studied with her uncle Saint Beuno, but one day, Prince Caradoc was out hunting and saw Winefride who was renowned for her beauty. He wanted to marry her but she refused his advances. He pursued her to the church but before she got into it, Caradoc caught her and in a fit of rage chopped off her head with his sword. Immediately a well sprang up from the earth where her severed head lay gushing with water for life and healing. St. Beuno, picked up her head, and put it back on her body as he prayed over her. Seeing the murderer leaning on his sword with an insolent and defiant air, St. Beuno cursed Caradoc and he not only dropped dead, but the ground opened and swallowed him.

Once healed Winefride took vows and established a community of women which possibly became a double monastery where both men and women could lead a monastic life. The gushing artesian spring at Holywell became known as a place of healing for body, mind and spirit and pilgrims still come to bathe themselves with the water. Some call it the Lourdes of Wales.

Saint Winefride is often depicted with a fountain at her feet and a red ring around her neck depicting the scar from her wounding which also became a sign of her healing. The red ring connects her both to Caradog, the agent of violence, and to Saint Beuno, who serves as an instrument of healing and God's grace.[41]

All of us bear scars that recall both wounding and healing. I am sure that Elizabeth did. Suddenly pregnant with what must have been a menopausal baby, she secluded herself from her community. She bore the scar of childlessness and the condemnation that went with it. Even her late pregnancy would have caused scars. Healing though it was to finally have a child, her advanced age must brought its own forms of rejection. Mary came to her for comfort, but her presence must also have been both comforting and healing to Elizabeth.

Reflection

Perhaps you too bear the scars of wounding and/or healing that have marred your life. As we walk though Advent towards the healing presence of Jesus you might like to take time to recall some of those scars - both the wounding and the healing. What stories do the scars tell? Write down one of the stories. Who were the agents of wounding? Who were the agents of healing in your life? Offer a prayer of forgiveness if necessary for those who wounded you. Give thanks for those who helped bring healing.[42]

God who is above us,
God who is beneath us,
God who is on every side,
Bring healing to our bodies.
God who is in the air,
God who is in the earth,
God who is in all creation,
Bring healing to our souls.
God who is beside us,
God who is within us,
God who never leaves us,
Bring healing for our wounds.
Make us whole.

Week 4 —
Searching for Peace

December 4th — Building the Community with St. Columba

Hope of all hopes, dream of our dreams,
*   a child is born, sweet-breathed; a son is given to us: a living gift.*
And even now, with tiny features and dewy hair, He is great.
*   The power of leadership, and the weight of authority, will rest on His*
shoulders.
His name? His name we'll know in many ways—
*   He will be called Wonderful Counselor, Mighty God,*
Dear Father everlasting, ever-present never-failing,
*   Master of Wholeness, Prince of Peace.*
[7] His leadership will bring such prosperity as you've never seen before—
*   sustainable peace for all time.*
This child: God's promise to David—a throne forever, among us,
*   to restore sound leadership that cannot be perverted or shaken.*
He will ensure justice without fail and absolute equity. Always.
*   The intense passion of the Eternal, Commander of heavenly armies,*
*   will carry this to completion.* (Isaiah 9:6,7 The Voice)

In his important book, *Living Toward a Vision: Biblical Reflections on Shalom,* Walter Brueggemann talks about the Biblical concept of peace. He explains that the original meaning of shalom was far more than the usual English translation *peace. Wholeness* or *completeness*[43] are better translations, but even these words are inadequate. In essence *shalom* is far more than the absence of conflict or even the existence of "inner peace". "Shalom is the substance of the Biblical vision of one community embracing all creation. It refers to all those resources and factors which make communal harmony joyous and effective."[44] It embraces God and God's desire to restore every part of creation and all aspects of life to the wholeness and harmony of relationship that was broken before humankind turned away from God. This is the kind of peace that comes when the entire creation is reconciled and once more lives in wholeness and harmony that we will focus on this week.

God believes in reconciliation – not just our inner transformation and reconciliation to God but also restoration of creation, the making of peace wherever there is enmity, healing wherever there is brokenness, and renewal wherever the image of God is distorted. Our creator has begun a process of redemption to restore all things to what they were meant to be.

Peace like this seemed to be central to Celtic spirituality. The love of creation, the concern for the poor, hospitality to friend and stranger, the embrace of unity in the midst of strife were all highlighted in the lives of the ancient Celtic saints.

We see it particularly in the life of Columba of Iona, banished from Ireland because of the violent conflict he caused, but repentant and humbled by this disaster. He was already known as a great diplomat, but also became a reconciler and peacemaker. He bridged a gap between the fledgling Christian culture and the pagan, druidic culture of his time. It was not an easy task, and the alliance had tense and difficult moments. He reminds us that the path towards peace and reconciliation is never easy. He was successful in reaching that harmony and unity through which Celtic Christianity flourished for many years.

There are many stories I love about this incredible man who loved to study, pray and write. He is reputed to have healed many during his travels and expelled numerous spirits and monsters. On one trip he evidently encountered the Loch Ness monster which had aggressively attacked a local person. He raised his holy hand, invoked the name of God, formed the saving sign of the cross in the air and commanded the ferocious creature to be gone and it fled. Even strangers were astounded and gave glory to the God of the Christians. [45]

The problems faced by Columba were similar to those that underly the conflicts of cultures in our world today and probably similar to those faced by Mary and Joseph as they travelled to Bethlehem compelled by the Roman Empire to attend the census. I wonder what kind of vision of peace they held in their hearts as they contemplated the child they would give birth to who would be called the Prince of Peace. I wonder if it occurred to them that he would one day clash with Rome's unyielding power, unable to reconcile their thirst for power and control with the message of God's peace that he would preach.

Reflection

What vision of peace do you hold in your heart as we head towards Christmas? Is it this vision of God's wholeness and shalom that is the Biblical dream fulfilled in the birth of Jesus Christ? Read the scripture above through several times. Close your eyes and imagine what you think God's new world will look like. What is the dream, fulfilled in the birth of Christ that fills your mind?

Where have you seen peace-making in action in the world, in your community, family and within yourself personally? Who are the people in your life that are peacemakers and help reinforce your impressions of the peace towards which God is leading us?

Is our world broken
Beyond repair?
Will we always meet violence
With more violence?
Death with death?
Hate with hate?
What has happened to love,
And the call to care for others
As we do ourselves?
What have we done with Jesus,
The One who holds it all together,
And promises to fix
All the broken and dislocated pieces
Of the universe.
The One who told us

Love your enemies,
Let them bring out the best in you,
Not the worst.
Live out your God created identity
Live generously and graciously towards others.
Be loving in all circumstances.
Shout out for justice where wrong is done.
Tread lightly on the earth
Care for creation.
Join God in kingdom work.
Enable all life to flourish.

December 5th — St. Patrick Peace through the Trinity

Go out and make disciples in all the nations. Ceremonially wash them through baptism in the name of the triune God: Father, Son, and Holy Spirit. (Matthew 28:19 The Voice)

A few years ago, when we celebrated Trinity Sunday, just after Easter, I decided to look for flowers and leaves with a tripartite structure that reflected the three in one nature of the Trinity – God is One in three – Creator, Redeemer and Breath of Life. It was a great deal of fun and emphasized for me yet again how much we miss out on when we don't know how to connect the glory of creation to the story of our faith.

The most familiar trinitarian symbol is the Irish shamrock, with its three-lobed leaves, which according to legend, St. Patrick pointed out to the Irish as a symbol of the true Trinitarian God who he preached to them about, and in whose name he blessed nature to sanctify it. Whether or not Patrick did actually use the shamrock to teach, the implication that the triune presence of God can be found all around us throughout the natural world, is very much in keeping with Celtic spirituality.

There are lots of other plants that bear the Trinity symbolism, many of them with three-petaled flowers like Trillium grandiflorum, a native of north-eastern and north-western U.S. It is also known as the Trillium lily because it is said to symbolize the Trinity. Both its flower and leaves are tripartite. Even that great healing plant, the aloe, known as a miracle plant because of its many uses, can be seen as a symbol of the Trinity. Its Trinity symbolism refers to the characteristic successive emergence of new foliage spears from the base of young plants in groups of three – first two beginning spears, and then a third one between them – reflecting the emergence of the Holy Spirit from our Creator and the Son in the interior of the Trinity. Talk about wonderful imagery for us to meditate on.

The trinitarian nature of God was particularly important for Celtic Christians who embraced the Trinity as a community or family —a perfect harmony of relationship. They reasoned that since the essential nature of God is love, and because it is impossible to practice love in isolation, God the Trinity must be a model of perfect community - three persons bound in a unity of love and peace. This trinitarian perspective was reflected in their art and their poetry. We saw it on the first week in the trinity knot composed of three equal interlaced arcs with a never-ending unbroken line, representing equality, eternity & unity, and peace. As I mentioned, its points are said to represent the Holy Trinity of the Creator, Redeemer & Breath of God.

More than that, each human family unit (be it family, clan or tribe) was seen as an icon of the Trinity. As I wrote that today my thoughts turned to the holy family - Joseph, Mary and Jesus a family unit, an icon of the Trinity. Even before Jesus was born, from the Celtic perspective, our trinitarian God was manifested in the family he would become a part of.

Irish poet, author and philosopher John O'Donahue expresses this beautifully in his book *Anam Cara*. "Friendship is the nature of God. The Christian concept of god as Trinity is the most sublime articulation of otherness and intimacy, an interflow of friendship."[46]

For the Celts, the Trinity was never inaccessible but a very real presence in all aspects of life and creation, an almost tangible Comforter and Protector who could ward off evil forces. It was always to the Three-as-One, the One-in-Three that prayer is made and as I read the wonderful Trinitarian prayers left to us through the great work of Alexander Carmichael and Douglas Hyde, I see this repeated over and over.

I love how easily the Celtic people spoke of the Trinity finding analogies not only in nature but also in family and daily life as in this prayer from Ireland.

Three folds of the cloth, yet one napkin is there,
Three joints in the finger, but still one finger fair.
Three leaves of the shamrock, yet no more than one shamrock to wear,
Frost, snow-flakes and ice, all in water their origin share,
Three persons in God; to one God alone we give prayer.[47]

When I shared this prayer at a seminar a couple of years ago one woman got very excited. The joints in her little finger were stiff and when she tried to do needlepoint it would not do what she wanted which made her frustrated and irritable. However this prayer changed her perspective. Now every time her finger restricts her action she is reminded of the Trinity and the importance of God's presence in her life.

Reflection

Water comes in three forms - steam, water and ice. Without it life would not exist. But we don't just need it in its liquid form, we need it in all forms. Without the icecaps, our sea levels would rise rapidly. Without the humidity that water particles in the air create many plants and animals would die. Take some ice cubes out of your freezer and place them in a small saucepan. Heat them on your stove. Watch them melt and come to the boil and form steam. Reflect on the Trinity while you do so.

Alternatively go for a walk and look for trinity related images in your garden or community. Take some pictures on your phones to help you recall the Trinity in the midst of our everyday lives. When you get home journal about what you learned about the presence of the Trinity in every aspect of life and of the world around you.

Maybe you would like to use this prayer to aid your reflections.

God with me lying down,
God with me rising up,
God with me in each ray of light,
Nor I a ray of joy without him,
Nor one ray without him.

Christ with me sleeping,
Christ with me waking,
Christ with me watching,
Every day and night,

Every day and night.

God with me protecting,
The Lord with me directing,
The Spirit with me strengthening,
For ever and for evermore
Ever and evermore, Amen.
Chief of Chiefs, Amen. [48]

December 6th — Peace through Community with St. David

Look at how good and pleasing it is
when families live together as one!
It is like expensive oil poured over the head,
running down onto the beard—
Aaron's beard!—
which extended over the collar of his robes.
It is like the dew on Mount Hermon
streaming down onto the mountains of Zion,
because it is there that the Lord has commanded the blessing:
everlasting life. (Psalm 133 CEB)

According to Esther de Waal, "The Celtic journey was never made alone. Celtic spirituality is corporate spirituality with a deep sense of connectedness to the earth itself and the natural elements, to the human family, not only the present immediate family into which each of us is born, but the extended family that stretches back in time through the many generations. In today's society, which increasingly likes to treat us as isolated units, and which seems to encourage an individualistic and competitive approach to life, the Celtic tradition brings another set of values."[49]

The Celts felt very comfortable with a God whose very nature was portrayed as a community of the One in Three and Three in One. They embraced this companionable relationship between persons and consequently were strongly committed to community life. As Esther de Waal expresses it "A God who is Trinity in unity challenges self-centred isolation and points instead to fellowship." They were very aware that to come into the presence of God meant to be drawn into community not just with the Trinity but with the entire human family and even into unity with God's creation. It meant to enter into fellowship with sisters and brothers from every tribe and nation – rich and poor, young and old, disabled and whole. It meant to identify with the sick, the oppressed and the marginalized.

We all need community. Tom and I live in a small intentional community in Seattle. We inhabit the middle floor of a triplex with a family in the apartment above and three singles in the basement apartment below. We share meals at least once a week, and garden together once a month. We love hospitality and enjoy entertaining guests from around the world. I love this richly diverse global culture of which I am a part and learn so much from my interactions with those of different cultures, ethnicities and ages.

I also grew up in a diversity of cultures. My father was Greek, my mother Scottish, my country Australia. As a young doctor, I moved to New Zealand and then to the Mercy Ship M/V Anastasis visiting 56 countries during my 12 years on the ship. Finally after Tom and I were married, settled in my forever home in Seattle. My faith has been shaped, reshaped and renewed by the diversity of my friends and colleagues. Today, I don't even need to travel or have others come to visit to experience this diversity. It is all around me. Our local community is richly diverse. There is a Muslim mosque less than a mile away, homeless people on our corners, retirement communities and yuppy villages.

All of these cultures provide rich learning experiences. But sometimes that journey across the street is harder than the one around the world. I make time for our international visitors but find it harder to take time for my neighbours. I am not always ready to have my mind stretched and my horizons broadened by those I meet.

Saint David, the patron saint of Wales, calls us to be mindful of the small, hidden acts of everyday life that weave together human community. As a young boy David was sent to a bishop's family to be fostered. This was common in prominent families of the time. Fostering helped form inter-community networks and create interdependent social ties that strengthened the whole community. He founded 12 monasteries, the last of which was at the site of the present day town of St. David in south west Wales.

David lived simply but treated others with respect and kindness. His words and his way of life encouraged others to join his communities and it is this emphasis on community that continues to influence Christianity in Wales. [50]

I often wonder about the community that Mary and Joseph travelled with to Bethlehem. It was probably a large caravan like the one in the story of Jesus as a twelve year old being left in Jerusalem, his parents not noticing his absence because the caravan was so large. Were they embraced by their companions and extended family? Did the women sit around the fire at night listening to Mary's story and sharing stories of their own pregnancies? Or did they ostracize and shun her and refuse to listen to the stories of angels and miracle conceptions? Was there an excitement about this child?

Reflection

Sit quietly for a few minutes and think about God's wonderfully diverse global community of which you are a part. Remind yourself of the friends and family who form your community. Now think about people of other cultures and faiths who have impacted your life. Thank God for the richness of your faith that has grown through the witness of others. What opportunities continue to provide meaningful interaction not just with friends but also with people of other faiths and cultures?

God build community,
From brokenness and indifference,
Build love and caring,
For you our beloved God,
For others in our world,
For your beautiful creation.

God build community.
From self-centredness and independence,
Build friendship and compassion,
For each other,
For the marginalized,
The abandoned and despised.

God build community.
From mistrust and misunderstanding,
Build unity and togetherness,
For all peoples, religions and nations.
God build community.
For our neighbours near and far,
For the earth and all creation.

December 7th — Peace through Friendship with St. Ciarán

The heart is delighted by the fragrance of oil and sweet perfumes, and in just the same way, the soul is sweetened by the wise counsel of a friend. (Proverbs 27:9 The Voice)

A special friend who accompanies us through all the ups and downs of life's journey is more precious than gold. Early Irish Christians called this person the anam cara. Anam is the Gaelic word for soul; cara is the word for friend.[51]

"Soul friend," or "anam cara," had the specific meaning of an intimate bond where two people opened their hearts to one another, sharing their doubts and fears, their struggles and successes, encouraging one another on the journey. It called for active listening, speaking when necessary but always out of a knowledge of who the other person was and what they needed. John O'Donahue, in his book *Anam Cara,* explains "With your anam cara, you could share your innermost self, your mind and your heart. This friendship was an act of recognition and belonging. When you had an anam cara, your friendship cut across all convention, morality and category. You were joined in an ancient and eternal way with the *'friend of your soul.'*" [52]

Stories abound of soul friendships from the Celtic saints. St. Brigid, for instance, required the practice of her followers. When overhearing a young man mention that his anam cara had died she insisted that he find another one immediately, "A person without a soul friend is like a body without a head," she famously remarked.

These relationships often flourished regardless of differences in age or gender and persisted even if the participants became separated by great distances, or, as in one delightful account involving Ciarán of Clonmacnoise and Kevin of Glendalough, even by death.

In 6th century Ireland, Ciarán stood out among a very illustrious crowd. While still a young man, he founded a significant monastery at Clonmacnoise. Kevin was just as gifted but his calling was expressed more modestly, gaining renown as a person of great holiness and prayer who established Glendalough in the Wicklow Mountains. Although differing in style and ambition, these two saints formed a strong soul friendship.

While in his early 30s, Ciarán fell ill, probably from the plague, and died. The brothers laid his body in the little church until his anam cara could arrive from Glendalough. Kevin entered the church, dismissed the others in attendance, and, as he prayed, the spirit of Ciarán returned to his body. The two conversed for a while then shared the Eucharist and exchanged gifts. After a brief time, Kevin emerged and declared that the body of his friend was ready for burial.

There is no substitute for being physically present with another person as a companion on the journey, and the Celtic saints often travelled across dangerous terrain to be together. Kevin made the arduous journey some 90 miles to Clonmacnoise and Ciarán's spirit even re-animated his body so their friendship could be fully realized. But the mystical elements of this story suggest that there is something going on beyond the physical. After his death, Ciarán existed in a liminal space, a reality beyond that bound by space and time. This "virtual reality" invites us to imagine new possibilities for spiritual growth and engagement. Once again John O'Donahue gives us the words to express this mystical experience. He suggests that when people care deeply for each other an ancient belonging awakens and discovers itself. "In friendship, an ancient circle closes. That which is ancient between you will mind you, shelter you and hold you together." 53

According to the Celtic Christians, Jesus had an anam cara in the apostle John "the loved disciple" who was one of his intimate circle of three special friends. He is also sometimes referred to as the foster brother of Jesus or foster son of Mary because Jesus commended Mary into his care at his death.

I have two very good friends who are life long anam caras, supporting, counselling, advising me. It is a mutual relationship that we all very much cherish. It makes me wonder about Mary. Was Elizabeth an anam cara for her? Was that why Mary raced to see her when she found out

107

she was pregnant? Was Elizabeth the one who mentored, supported and encouraged her through this difficult time? What do you think?

Reflection

Do you have an anam cara? Is there a friend or a mentor who has supported and mentored you throughout your life? Sit quietly and think about the friends that surround you. Does one stand out as an anam cara, a special friend who has encouraged, supported and mentored you? How could you strengthen that relationship to make it an even closer one? If you don't have a close friend like this is there someone who could potentially become that friend to you?

Unite us God Almighty,
Unite us with the threefold cord of friendship.
Unite us with the threefold cord of love.
In the name of the Creator,
In the name of the Son,
In the name of the Spirit,
Unite us with the Three,
Unite us with the One,
Unite us with the strands
That can never be broken.

December 8th — Peace through Circling Prayers

God of Zion, to you even silence is praise.
Promises made to you are kept—
you listen to prayer—
and all living things come to you. (Psalm 61: 1,2 CEB)

The Blessing to the Four Directions is a beautiful form of prayer that has its roots in Native American culture. It is centered on the belief that human beings are tied to all things in nature. It is this belief which assigned virtues to the four cardinal directions; East, South, West and North. When one prays to the four directions, it is a way to call in Spirit through the unique energies of the directions. It is also a prayer that is resonant with the Celtic Caim Prayer, or the encircling prayer. This is a way of praying that calls in the Sacred Presence that is all around us, and literally asks for the Spirit to be present at the front, back, sides— even above and below—of an individual. It is a prayer of protection and sets the expectation that our Creator God will be present as both a shield of protection, and the intention that one will now move through the day in a sacred rhythm.[54]

I was first introduced to this form of prayer by a friend who stopped on a bridge during his morning walk to work to pray. He would face east, the direction of the sunrise and the Cascade mountains, representing the birth of new things and he prayed for students and the new ideas they were absorbing. He faced south towards the Duwamish River, as this direction often represents water, and prayed for the ecosystem in which he lived, especially for the waterways, on which so much work is currently being done to reverse pollution. Then he faced west looking over the city of Seattle, the direction of the sunset, often representing the harvest of hard work, and prayed for all those who were at work in it. Then he looked north towards Canada where he was born, often considered the direction of the ancestors and the elders, where we look for wisdom, inner healing and spiritual insight and prayed for the spiritual life of the city, that it would become a light to those that worked and lived in it. Finally, he looked inward and prayed for his own spiritual growth and discernment and the wisdom to be a spiritual guide to those he taught.

My friend Mary DeJong, often uses this kind of prayer in the form of a circling prayer, also known as Caim prayer (from the Irish gaelic meaning 'protection'). These are used to create a ring of safety around one's self and ones beloveds. It is a great way to pray within the physical dimension as it requires the body to actively participate in the pleas of the heart. The invocation begins with an arm extended, one finger pointing towards the ground, tracing the shape of a circle. This intentional act creates a sacred sphere, a space within which the pray-er invokes the protection of the divine. When we pray a Caim, we can extend these boundaries beyond our personal reach to include our whole house, neighborhood, the community in which we live, and the world at large. We encircle a space much larger than ourselves as a way to include the vast and diverse community of life of which we are a part.

By extending the Caim protection beyond our person to include plants, trees, birds, and other wildlife, we do something different than invoking a defense against that which is forbidden, dangerous, or out of control; instead, we invite that wild world in, bringing the more-than-human community of life into revered relationship and atunement. We invite a way of seeing the wild as wondrous and awe inspiring, seeing ourselves within its ward. Encircling prayers that cast the boundaries beyond our domesticated borders initiate a way of moving through the day that is expectant of mystery and magic as the whole of creation is considered to be within the Caim circle. In this way, Caim prayers become an eco-centric way of praying.

Mary also expanded this form of prayer into a prayer of Seven directions, including the directions of up (Cosmos), down (Earth), and within (Soulscape). I love this expanded prayer, it is a way not only to centre ourselves on the Divine presence, but also to embrace the entirety of creation and our place within it. This expands the prayerful imagination to include the universal principals of diversity, particularity, interiority, and communion. It honors the indigenous tradition of knowing that God's presence is as diverse and particular as the directions, and invites the supplicant to ground their prayers in a place.

110

She calls this the "The Rewilding Wheel Seven Directions Prayer" She explains: "It is a prayer that honors the rhythm of our days, the sacredness found within the seasons, and how that is reflected through our life's journey. It also provides a way to speak an authentic land acknowledgment, honoring with respect the traditional tribal lands upon which we live."

Reflection

Find a place outside where you can practice this form of the *Caim* with your whole being and all your senses. Back yards, front gardens, public parks, and even sidewalks will do! Just don't stand in the middle of the street!

Centre yourself by taking several deep slow breaths, in through your nose and out through your mouth, tuning in to the sounds of the natural world all around you. Don't be distracted by traffic noises or planes overhead. Receive all the sounds, natural as well as human-made, as an invitation to include them in your *Caim* too.

When you feel ready, position your body facing north. Breath deeply and feel the air within and around you. Stretch out your arm in front of you with your pointer finger extended and pointed to draw a metaphorical, expansive circle that includes the natural world. Slowly turn your body in a clock-wise rotation--going from the cardinal direction north, to east, to south, to west and back again to facing north while saying this simple encircling prayer, adapted to include the greater community of things with whom we live:

- North, "Circle us Spirit, Keep protection near, And danger afar."
- East, "Circle us Spirit, Keep light near, And darkness afar."
- South, "Circle us Spirit, Keep peace within, Keep evil out."
- West, "Circle us Spirit, Keep hope within, Keep doubt without."
- Back at the North can finish your prayers with: May you be a bright flame before us, May you be a guiding star above us, May you be a smooth path below us, And a loving Guide behind us, Today, tonight, and forever.

Amen.[55]

Creator God,
I rest in the circle of your love,
And am filled with the wonder of your presence.
Redeemer Christ,
I rest in the circle of your forgiveness,
And know the joy of being washed clean.
Sustainer Spirit,
I rest in the circle of your guidance,
And am counseled by your wisdom.
God who is One, God who is Three,
You draw all life into the sacred circle
Of your Eternal embrace.
Let us rest within this circle of new life,
And walk the path of your leading.

December 9th — Peace through the Angels with St. Columba

This is how the birth of Jesus Christ took place. When Mary his mother was engaged to Joseph, before they were married, she became pregnant by the Holy Spirit. Joseph her husband was a righteous man. Because he didn't want to humiliate her, he decided to call off their engagement quietly. As he was thinking about this, an angel from the Lord appeared to him in a dream and said, "Joseph son of David, don't be afraid to take Mary as your wife, because the child she carries was conceived by the Holy Spirit. (Matt 1:18-20 CEB)

When on Iona, one of the places I love to stop and sit and pray is what is known as the Hill of the Angels. It is about half way across the island towards the western beach known as the machair, a small hill from which you can see the sea in both directions. Evidently St. Columba came here each day to pray. He went alone and forbad the monks to follow him. One day, however, a curious monk wondering why Columba seemed so secretive about his visits, followed him and hid himself on the other side of the hill. From there he could see Columba standing on a knoll praying with his arms spread toward heaven. Suddenly he saw angels flying down from heaven dressed in white robes. They gathered round Columba as he prayed and conversed with him. After awhile they returned to the heavens.

After his conference with the angels, Columba returned the monastery and aware that he had been spied on reproached the monks for their disobedience. The guilty monk came forward and asked for forgiveness. Columba took him aside and sternly charged him not to tell anyone about his angelic vision as long as Columba was alive. After Columba's death the monk testified publicly to this visitation.[56]

This story is reminiscent of the Biblical account of Jacob in Genesis 28:11-17 where he dreams of a ladder up to heaven with angels ascending and descending. Angels appear to Abraham, to Hagar, to Lot and to many others throughout the Bible. Angels are very much a part of the Jewish faith. The Celts too were very aware of the angels that surrounded them coming both as messengers and as guardians, creating ladders and threshold places to the heavenly realm. They knew the thin places where these encounters were more likely to happen, as we see in the story of Columba and often invoked their wisdom and protection.

To be honest I never paid much attention to these angelic visitors until I read Christine Valters Paintner's book *The Love of Thousands.* She comments that in the Celtic tradition, though there is no direct portal to the supernatural realm, there are moments when the doorway appears, and we are able to experience a connection to the sacred in a more concrete way than in ordinary time. There are openings that break through our everyday vision so we can see angels at work in our world.[57] Valters Paintner talks about our need to be attentive, take time, honour mutuality and nourish trust in our relationship with angels, both the messengers or archangels and the guardian angels that surround all of us.

Angels are one of those remarkable aspects of our world that tell us the veil between heaven and earth is not as impenetrable as we think it is. All around us, the unseen world is constantly interacting with our world in ways that we can become aware of if we allow ourselves to.

Angels figure quite prominently in the Advent and Christmas story. In fact they frame the story. It is the angel Gabriel who comes to Mary to tell her she will become pregnant and bear a son. Gabriel also appears to Zechariah to announce that his wife too will have a child, Then Joseph is visited by angels, not just those that told him to go ahead and marry Mary, but also before the flight into Egypt and then again when it is time to return. He must have been a very spiritually attuned person, constantly surrounded by the angelic hosts.

My favourite encounter with angels is at the birth of Christ when a glorious chorus of angels fills the sky singing "peace on Earth", announcing to the shepherds that Christ the Messiah has been born. I always feel that there was so much excitement in heaven at the birth of this child that the angels could not contain themselves and had to break into the earthly realm with their announcement. One gets the feeling that this heavenly host is always watching our world, invisibly encouraging us and supporting us, ready to appear when needed, watching in expectation that the fulfillment of God's dream for peace and harmony will be fulfilled.

Reflection

Circling prayers can be used in so many situations and are ideally suited to our interactions with angels. Sit quietly in your sacred space and take some deep breaths in and out. Draw an imaginary circle around you and imagine it is God's circle of protection that embraces not just you but also the angels that guard, protect and guide you. Read thought this prayer 3 times. Close your eyes and bask in the encircling presence of the angels.

The holy Apostles' guarding,
The gentle martyrs' guarding,
The nine angels' guarding,
Be cherishing me, be aiding me.

The quiet Brigit's guarding,
The gentle Mary's guarding,
The warrior Michael's guarding,
Be shielding me, be aiding me.

The God of the elements' guarding,
The loving Christ's guarding,
The Holy Spirit's guarding,
Be cherishing me, be aiding me. [58]

December 10th — St. Piran Makes Peace with Creation

Wolf and lamb will graze together,
* and the lion will eat straw like the ox,*
* but the snake — its food will be dust.*
They won't hurt or destroy at any place on my holy mountain,
* says the Lord.* (Isaiah 65:25 CEB)

One of my favourite legends about the Celtic Saints involves St. Piran, the most famous of the saints said to have come from Ireland to Cornwall. When he arrived he sat down under a tree with a wild boar. At first the boar fled in terror, but then sensing Piran's great love for all God's creatures, it returned to become Piran's servant. Tearing branches and grass with its teeth, the boar built Piran a simple cell in which he could live. Soon other animals came out of the forest to join them. A fox, a badger, a wolf and a doe, all quite tame, with Piran as their abbot.

One day the fox stole Piran's shoes, renounced his vows and carried them to his lair to chew on them. Piran sent the badger after the fox and seeing the fox about to eat his master's shoes, bit his ears and tail and pulled the fox back to the monastery. "Why have you committed this crime, dear brother something that a monk should never do?" Piran asked. The fox begged Piran's forgiveness, did penance, fasted and refused to eat until Piran gave permission. After that all the animals lived in peace bound together by devotion for their abbot. [59]

Fanciful, maybe, but it shows the wonderful relationship that many of the Celtic Saints had with animals. The Celts understood the physical world as an expression of God - God's essence was breathed into every creature in the same way it was into the first human being. Because of this, they respected and cared for all animals which were often drawn to them as a result.

So what of the essence of God comes to us through the created world? Dogs can teach us about the sense of smell. Owls can teach us about sight, but the most incredible lesson I learnt recently came from the plant world. We tend to think of trees as individual units, but they are actually part of a large, interconnected community interacting with their own and other species, including forming kin relationships with their genetic relatives. I can imagine that the tree of life in the garden of Eden was like this, connected not just to other trees in the garden but to all the vegetation that made up the garden, sharing wisdom, encouraging growth and keeping healthy.

Suzanne Simard, Canadian scientist and Professor in the Department of Forest and Conservation Sciences at the University of British Columbia, and author of *The Mother Tree*, explains that sometimes an ancient mother tree is connected to hundreds of young saplings which they communicate with and help sustain through the fungal network that is part of the forest. What she calls "the Wood Wide Web" is a busy network, where the fungal links serve as pathways for the back-and-forth transport of carbon, water, and nutrients among trees. Among the shifting dynamics of growing trees, the taller, replete, and illuminated elders can shuttle a net amount of resources along a source-sink gradient to shorter, shaded, understory trees.[60]

Don't you love this imagery? Nothing teaches us more about God's intention for an interconnected, mutually supportive world than this. Mary and Joseph lived in a world of greater connectivity to nature than we do today. Two thousand years ago Palestine was heavily forested with oaks, sycamore and pine in many places. I wonder if they too were aware of the essence of God present in these beautiful trees.

Reflection

Is there a stand of big trees, a forest or a beautiful garden near you that you could go and stand in for a few minutes? Take some deep breaths in and out, close your eyes and breathe in the fragrance of it, the rich loamy smell of the forest floor, the layers of mulch protecting the plants.

Imagine those fungal filaments that reach out between each tree, communicating, nurturing, supporting. What does this teach you about the character of God?

There is wonder in the world,
We cannot comprehend,
Miracles of light and beauty,
Mystery of things that grow
In the depths of night.
No science can explain the splendour,
Or help us understand
When sunset colours
Take our breath away,
And bring us to tears.
Why do strangers show compassion,
For people half a world away,
And care when violence
Rips society apart?
Why do we ache
When forests are destroyed,
And species made extinct,
As though the spark of God
Is snuffed out?
This world is alive with God.
Filled with the essence of our creator.
Divine love shimmers through creation.
All is infused with holy presence,
Filled with love and life and beauty.

Week 5 — Joy

In the Journey

December 11th — The Joy of Cooking with St. Ciarán

On this mountain,
the Lord of heavenly forces will prepare for all peoples
a rich feast, a feast of choice wines,
of select foods rich in flavor,
of choice wines well refined. (Isaiah 25:6 CEB)

By this fifth week of Advent I am usually in the midst of an orgy of Christmas baking. We love to entertain friends lavishly during this season and those that can't come to visit often receive packages in the mail. The rich aroma of shortbread, English fruitcake, lemon bars, and chocolate ginger cookies fills my house every day as I bake and enter the delight of preparing for Christmas hospitality.

Baking is relaxing for me, an activity filled with joy as I anticipate the friends and family I will share everything with. So appropriate for this fifth week of Celtic Advent, the third of traditional Advent whose theme is joy. On Sunday, at the beginning of the week, we light the pink Joy candle on our traditional Advent wreath. It is pink because rose is a liturgical color for joy. The third Sunday of Advent is Gaudete Sunday and is meant to remind us of the joy that the world experienced at the birth of Jesus.

There are many stories about food, hospitality and even baking told about the Celtic saints. The one I love is about St. Ciarán when he was at Clonard. Evidently the school went through a time of famine and the grain being taken to the local mill for grinding needed to be protected by one of the monks. When it was Ciarán's turn to take the oats he prayed "O Lord, I would like this to be beautiful wheat, that it would bring great, pleasant, and delightful satisfaction to the elders." God sent an angel to the mill while Ciarán was singing his psalms and the

120

oats that were being ground were changed so that when they came out, they were choice wheat.

When the grinding of the grain was finished, that one sack of oats had become four sacks of consecrated wheat. Ciarán took it home and baked bread for the elders, the best they had ever eaten. Its taste was so good with both mead and wine that it satisfied and healed them all. Every sick person in the monastery who ate the bread became at once perfectly whole. [61]

Sometimes I feel that my baking too is touched by the angels of God to gain a special flavour that is reminiscent of the heavenly food God fed the Hebrews in the desert. As I share it, I often wonder if I am actually sharing with angels unawares.

As I bake I often reflect on the joy of the Advent season and what it means to me. I imagine Mary and Joseph journeying towards Bethlehem, she heavily pregnant, he a concerned and anxious father to be, probably filled with a mixture of joy at seeing family and apprehension as to what kind of reception they might receive. I wonder if they had to leave home in a hurry like the Hebrews did when leaving Egypt. Did they pack provisions of unleavened bread, carrying their bread pans on their shoulders, wrapped in their robes, as described in Exodus 12:34? Did they carry the usual simple travel food of olives and lentils, chickpeas, and onions? Maybe they could afford almonds and pistachios, honey, figs dates and wine as well. The journey would have taken at least four days and I like to think that there was a festive mood throughout the caravan. Perhaps people sat around a fire at night sharing their provisions. After all this was a very hospitable culture. It is unlikely that anyone would have been uncared for and allowed to go hungry.

Reflection

Consider cooking a simple meal such as Mary and Joseph might have eaten on their journey. Pita bread, humus, olives, maybe figs and dates or other seasonal fruit. A few almonds and pistachio nuts as well. Accompany it with wine or water. During the meal talk about Mary and Joseph's walk to Bethlehem. What do you think it would have been like - the food, the company, the road? What dangers might they have faced? What would it have been like for a heavily pregnant woman? Christmas cards often show Mary on a donkey but it is more likely she that walked. What would that long trip have been like?

At the end of the meal you might like to share bread and wine or juice together in a blessing. Offer a small piece of your bread to your spouse, significant other or a friend, exchange whatever blessing you like. Then invite others at the meal to do the same.

Here's a simple blessing you can use, or you might like to create a unique blessing of your own:

Person offering the bread says: Remember throughout the year ahead that Christ, the living bread, is always with you.

Person receiving responds: And remember, every day, that I am here for you too.[62]

God today we gazed on the beauty of your world,
Enthralled by its splendour.
We baked bread,
From its abundant harvest,
Ate food from its fruit,
And cherished the gift of its food.
We drank in its wonder,
And were filled with the water of life.
Now we pause to give thanks,
And remember your generous hospitality.
We came into your dwelling place, O God,
And caught a glimpse of your holy mountain,
You gave us a foretaste of your eternal banquet,
A lavish feast, an invitation for all the people of the world.

December 12th — Joy in the Book Of Kells

The true light that shines on all people
was coming into the world.
The light was in the world,
and the world came into being through the light,
but the world didn't recognize the light. (John 1:9,10 CEB)

I will never forget my visit to the library at Trinity College Dublin. In a room kept dim to preserve it, a see-through case holds a masterpiece, one of the art wonders of the world. This is the Book of Kells, the richest and most lavishly illuminated manuscript of the four gospels in the Celtic style that still exists. It may have been created by St. Columba on the island of Iona, was probably removed by the monks when they fled the Viking raids and taken to the Abbey of Kells which itself was raided repeatedly. The fact that most of it survived is almost miraculous. It was stolen and buried for three months, then passed from family to family and place to place until Charles II presented it to Trinity College in 1661.

These illuminated manuscripts were special even at the time of their creation. Every copy of every book produced for many centuries was made in a monastery scriptorium. Monks everywhere could write well enough to make copies of documents, but not every monastery could undertake the production of copies of books, an activity that required specialist skills. Even fewer monasteries had the expertise and artistry to undertake the production of highly decorated books like The Book of Kells and others that still exist including The Book of Durrow and the Lindisfarne Gospels. It is no wonder that so much effort was made to preserve them.

The beauty, symbolism and artistry of Celtic illuminated manuscripts like the Book of Kells is breathtaking, something to marvel at, priceless artifacts that are a joy to look at. I can imagine the monks hunched over the vellum, pin pricking guidelines for the text; lettering verses with iron-gall ink; illuminating pages with costly pigments and gold leaf—still vibrant centuries later. Each one was composed of beautiful text, written in the most careful and elegant hand, along with intricate borders, of Celtic knot work, spiraling vines, interweaving images of animals and birds, some realistic, some twisted and fantastical all of it embellished, or *illuminated*, with shining sections of precious gold leaf.

The words IN PRINCIPIO ERAT VERBUM ET VERBUM "In the beginning was the Word, and the Word was with God," the opening words of the Gospel of John, is a particularly impressive opening to any piece of writing. The rich ornateness of the ornamentation captivates the eye and can hold one's attention for hours. Not surprising as The Gospel of John was the favourite of the Celtic Christians.

Probably the greatest joy of the Book of Kells are the illuminated initial letters scattered with generous abandon through every page of the text. Their whimsical nature gives a sense of the delight the monks must have found in crafting them. Even small letters in the middle of a line are embellished with an extra twirl filled with contrasting colours, and open spaces at the end of a sentence are filled with stars, or fish or birds. Maybe these speak of the fun-loving nature of the monks too.

Unfortunately the Advent story does not really feature in The Book of Kells, though Christmas does. There is only one depiction of a woman in the entire manuscript. It is the earliest surviving image of Mary and the Christ child in Western manuscript art. In contrast to the biblical description of Mary as a humble peasant, here she is depicted as an empress, enthroned and wearing royal clothing, an indication of how the impressions of her changed over the centuries. She is surrounded by four 'courtiers', in this case angels. Jesus is seated on her lap, with his hand placed on her clearly visible breast – an allusion to milk of Christian instruction, and also perhaps the fountain of life. The elaborate frame around the image is perhaps an allusion to its ultimate source.[63]

I love to paint on rocks, and at times have tried to copy some of the less intricate patterns of the Book of Kells onto my stones. First I create a pattern with pencil, a consuming process requiring much erasing and repositioning. Then I outline the pattern with my paint pens and lastly fill in the resulting design with vibrant colours. It is a process of joy, and gives me a little glimpse into the delight the monks must have felt as they worked on their far more elaborate illuminations.

Reflection

The Book of Kells can now be viewed online for free. Follow the link below and scroll down the images until you find one that catches your attention. Spend a few minutes gazing at the image. Let your eyes rest on the characters and objects. Note your feelings as you examine the whole of the work. Write down what you are sensing. Now look at the image again, particularly at the details of the intricate embellishments. Does something new catch your attention? Keep your eyes focused on that for a couple of minutes and allow God to speak to you through the image. Write down your impressions. End with prayer. [64]

God of every beautiful thing,
Give us eyes to see the wonder,
Of your world,
Let it disrupt our days with sacred pauses,
So that we marvel,
Not just at majestic mountains
And sweeping vistas,
But at the sparks of mystery
Carved in every ordinary thing,
That fills this earth
With your glory.
Let our hearts swell with delight,
At every wrinkled face made in God's image,
Let us glory in the divine light
Enlivening every humdrum moment,
With the joy of your presence.

December 13th — Exploring Joy with John O'Donahue

My heart is bursting with a new song;
lyrics to my king erupt like a spring
for my king, to my king;
my tongue is the pen of a poet, ready and willing. (Psalm 45:1 The Voice)

The Celtic Christian influence did not die out when the Roman church won the day at the council of Whitby. Sometimes hidden, sometimes very vocal, Celtic voices always added their music and poetry and writing to life and culture. Today there are a myriad of Celtic voices who bring new vitality and inspiration to our lives by connecting us to the Celtic tradition. The most prominent of these is John O'Donahue, poet, philosopher, and scholar who died in 2008, but whose books still profoundly influence my life and the lives of many others.

John O'Donahue had a unique ability to translate the Irish imagination into spiritual truths and is filled with a joy at the wonder of life and our world that continue to guide many followers of Jesus in their Christian journey. O'Donohue's first published work of prose, *Anam Cara*, catapulted him into a more public life as an author, speaker and teacher. He also devoted his energies to environmental activism, and his very Celtic love of God's beautiful creation comes through much of what he wrote.

The Invisible Embrace of Beauty is my favourite of his books. In it he encourages our greater intimacy with beauty, inspiring us to welcome its invisible embrace and inviting it to lead us towards new heights of passion and creativity. He comments "if your style of looking becomes beautiful, then beauty will become visible and shine forth for us.... When we beautify our gaze, the grace of hidden beauty becomes our joy and our sanctuary."[65] I love to imagine that everything in God's world is beautiful if we are able to beautify our gaze in order to really perceive it from God's perspective. Can you imagine how our perceptions of the world around us, the people we meet and God's good creation would change if we looked at everything with a "beautified gaze"?

In another part of the book he writes: "the very breath of life breathes into things until their individual colours flame. Such is the generosity of air, self-effacing and unseen it asks nothing of the eye, yet it offers life to the invisible fields where light can unfold its scriptures of colour. We dwell between the air and the earth, guests of that middle kingdom where light and colour embrace." [66]

As I contemplate this today, I am reminded that white light is not really white at all, it is made up of all the colours of the rainbow. I also recall that in Jesus' body too are all the colours of the rainbow. During Advent I often hunt for images of Christ and Christmas music from different cultures. There are Ethiopian icons, and black madonnas, He Qi's Chinese images[67] and Hanna Varghese's Malaysian images. Sometimes I deliberately look for unsettling images that really do make Advent unfamiliar again, like Kelly Latimore's icons of the Holy Family as refugees, and Jesus born in a homeless shelter and another of him born under the rubble of the war in Gaza[68], and the abbey altar piece know as The Visit of the Angels, painted between 1390 and 1400 of Mary knitting. Latimore's images are unsettling because they transport Jesus into the areas of conflict, abuse and violence in our world today. The altar cloth is unsettling because Mary is doing something mundane and everyday when the angels come to her.

I ponder these different images of Christ's birth and sit in awe of the rainbow hues that make up the light of Christ. I do feel I live in that place between the air and the earth, guests of that middle kingdom where light and colour embrace. I realize I will never appreciate the light of Christ until I fully embrace the colours of God's rainbow of joy that are all the tribes and nations and cultures, all social strata and sexual orientations of our earth. These kind of images connect me in a deeper way to the Advent story, coming of Christ and the richness of God's children "from every tribe and nation".

Reflection

Visit He Qi's and Kelly Latimore's websites or instagram accounts and/ or find some other images of Christ's birth and the Holy Family from different cultures. Choose 2 or 3 of these images to reflect on over the coming days. As you reflect on each image, let your eyes rest on the characters and objects. Note your feelings as you examine the whole of the work. Write down what you are sensing. Now look at the image again, particularly at the details of the painting and any embellishments that might decorate it. Does something new catch your attention? Keep your eyes focused on that for a couple of minutes and allow God to speak to you through the image. Write down your impressions. End with prayer.

Today's prayer was inspired by reading John O'Donahue's work.

Drink in the light of the world,
Let it fill you with joy.
Breathe in the wonder,
Of the way it dances
across the landscape,
Anointing each tree, each plant, each field,
With the spirit's blessed touch.
Watch it caress the leaves and flowers,
With its gentleness.
See it kiss the heads of children,
As they laugh and play.
Look up at the sky above
Touched by the morning sun,
Lacy clouds hang so high
They dwarf the planes that fly beneath.
God's delight whispers through its rays.
Holy love, glorious joy unbounded.

December 14th — Finding Joy in A Thin Place

Because of our God's deep compassion,
the dawn from heaven will break upon us,
to give light to those who are sitting in darkness
and in the shadow of death,
to guide us on the path of peace." (Luke 1:78,79 CEB)

We have talked a lot about how, for Celtic Christians, God was a key part of all things natural and beautiful. We have pondered how they praised God's design and creation of all things and reflected on how creation was seen as translucent with the glory of God shining through it. The hills, the sky, the sea, the forests were not God, but their spiritual qualities revealed God and were connected to God.

However, in some special places people felt a very strong connection to God's presence. In these places it often feels as though the veil that separates earth and heaven is lifted and inhabitants of both worlds can momentarily touch each other. These places are referred to as "thin places", where the space between the spirit world and the physical world becomes thin, sometimes translucent and a sense of the transcendence of God breaks through.

When Tom and I visited Iona several years ago we were very aware of the special nature of this place and the thinness of the veil that hung over all the island. Columba's beach, the Hill of the Angels, and the Abbey cloister in particular, all have a wonder about them that makes one sense that heaven is but a breath away. The waves of the ocean seem to whisper Jesus' words "I am with you always." In this, as in any hallowed space and time, heaven and earth for a moment seem as one.

We all have thin places in our lives, where we experience the presence of our Creator God, the presence of the Holy, as though that veil between heaven and earth evaporated. For some it is a special place in the mountains or by the ocean or watching a beautiful sunrise or sunset from a much loved vantage point. I believe we also have thin places in our regular lives. Things we do, or love that help us to experience the presence of God. We all need to allow ourselves, to give ourselves permission, to do more of those thin place things! You might experience thin place while working in the garden or baking bread. For some people it's through music, playing it or singing it. For others, their thin place is outdoors, running, hiking, even surfing! It might be in your creative outlet or in writing.

We usually return from thin places refreshed and renewed, aware that all of life has the potential to become a thin place where we experience the joy of intimacy with our Creator. Having experienced the glimpses of glory in those sacred landscapes, we begin to catch glimpses of it all around us. Soon the birds outside our window sing of the mystery we might have passed over in our busyness. Glowing sunsets crack open the door once more to the invisible realm, and as we sit in silence, we hear the divine rhythm of the ebb and flow of God's love.

We cannot spend all our lives in these thin places but we can often return to them in our memory and in our imagination. When I am overcome with small tedious details and endless tasks, I hold my serpentine rock picked up on Columba's beach, close my eyes and return to Iona. Sitting on Columba's pebbled beach, I hear again the silent music of angel voices and the abiding presence of God's love.

I wonder if Mary was sitting in a "thin place" when the angel Gabriel first came to her. Was this a special place she went to pray and seek God? Or was she engaged in mundane everyday activities whose rhythms drew her into the presence of God?

Reflection

Reflect on the thin places in your own life. Where is a place that refreshes your spirit and opens the door to the threshold of God's loving presence? Sit and prayerfully imagine yourself once more entering that place. What are some of the themes or life lessons which have emerged when you have previously entered this and other thin places in your own life? What new ideas and insights come to you as you once more sit and contemplate in this special place? Write down what you sense God is saying to you. Experience God's blessing and the wonder of God's peace as it flows over you. In what ways could you enable yourself to enter that thin place on a more regular basis?

Sometimes in a lowly cell
In the presence of my God
I stand and listen.
In the silence of my heart,
I can hear his will,
When I listen,
Despairing people flock to me
They expect that I can see
The answers
They ask my advice
They say I am wise.
I answer,
That nothing can deceive me
If I stand alone and silently listen,
For I am but a servant,
Who is guided by his king,
When I listen.
Sometimes in a lowly cell
In the presence of my God
I stand and listen. [69]

December 15th — The Joy of Naming on Iona

On the eighth day, it came time to circumcise the child. They wanted to name him Zechariah because that was his father's name. But his mother replied, "No, his name will be John." They said to her, "None of your relatives have that name." Then they began gesturing to his father to see what he wanted to call him. After asking for a tablet, he surprised everyone by writing, "His name is John." (Luke 1:59-63 CEB)

In his book *In Search of Sacred Places: Looking for Wisdom on Celtic Holy Islands*[70], Daniel Taylor mentions that everything on Iona has a name and comments that when we name things, we begin to value them. The names on Iona often tell the history of the island too. St. Columba, for example is said to have come ashore at what is now known as Columba's Bay. The hill behind the bay is called Cairn of the Back to Ireland, or Back Turned to Ireland. In other words, these Celtic saints knew they had come to stay and were deliberately turning their backs away from their beloved homeland.

Taylor comments "Everything on Iona has a name. each physical feature of the island has been part of a specific human experience and therefore thought worthy of bearing a name…. These many names are a testimony to the human scale of life on Iona. As the scale of physical size diminishes as one travels to the island - England, Scotland, Mull, Iona - the scale of individuals and spiritual significance increases. Walking is the maximum desirable speed for seeing things fully enough to name them. And when we name things we begin to value them. No wonder we want to be named and known."[71]

The name we know someone or something by really does matter, and unfortunately as landscapes get developed and habitats are destroyed, the names around us often hauntingly reflect a landscape and a people that no longer exist. Sometimes they are changed so that the history is forgotten or devalued, or we give them generic names – streets and houses with numbers not names and our primary landmarks are the mall and the commercial district, not the bay or the lake on which they are built. In fact those once upon a time landmarks may have been destroyed to give us our modern cities.

I suspect that when Adam named the animals in Genesis, each naming was an occasion for awe and wonder. I cannot imagine that he just gave them a generic "horse", "dog" "antelope" kind of name without forethought or consideration for what the animal was. My impression is that he sat and pondered each one. Looking closely, maybe examining the creature, seeing how it was created and then naming it. The more intimately he knew the animal the more certain he was of what to call it.

One advantage of the COVID lockdown was that it sent us out into our neighbourhoods where we learned the names of the shops and the landmarks that surround us, and sometimes of our neighbours, for the first time. We were awakened to the beauty and value of neighbourhoods and the people we live with and discovered the joy of knowing our surroundings well enough to value the names of our neighbours and our neighborhoods. By so doing, we not only learned to value what we saw, we also learned to value ourselves more as important elements in the midst of our environment as well. Many of us learned – I matter here, and now. I matter because of my connection to this place.

"We have stunned the world out of wonder" says Robert MacFarlane in his fascinating book *Landmarks*. He suggests that "once a landscape goes undescribed and therefore unregarded it becomes vulnerable to unwise use or improper action." He explains that when the moorland on the island of Lewis in Scotland was in danger of being converted into a major wind farm that would have permanently destroyed the countryside, the residents realized they faced a challenge. They needed to re-enchant people's perception of the moor so that it had intrinsic value. They mapped out the moor and its walking paths. They gathered poetry and songs from its history. They heightened people's awareness of the descriptive language of plants and landscape. Re-enchanting the moorland came through the naming of every detailed part of the moor. This gave it value in the sight not just of the islanders but of the whole country. And the moorland was saved.

What if I try to name each plant and tree that I pass on my morning walks, not just with the generic name of its species but with specific names that describe its beauty and its glory? The lilac bush outside my window becomes the fragrant purple flowered bush that fills my heart with delight. What if I ask the man who sits on the corner each day begging for money his name, and use his name imbuing him with dignity and respect?

In Jesus' day, a first son was usually given the same name as his father. Elizabeth and Mary both broke with tradition. Elizabeth named her son John, which means "God is gracious", not Zechariah. His name declares a new being from God, a new act of God. It is a break with John's father, and all his fathers. As the last of the Prophets, he is the true pivot of history, heralding the end of the Old Covenant and the arrival of a new era.

Mary too broke with tradition by calling her son Jesus, "God saves" not Joseph. Even though it was a fairly popular name at that time, I wonder if it raised eyebrows around the family and the village, but she too was declaring something new, a new beginning and the arrival of a new world in which God would, through this child, make all things whole again.

Reflection

Where in your life might God be calling you to re-enchant your perception? Perhaps it is in your attitude towards God. Or maybe it is your perception of yourself or those around you. Or perhaps you too need to re-enchant the landscape around you so that you see the beauty and wonder of it from God's perspective.

A good way to begin this re-enchantment is by considering your own name. Do you know its meaning? If not find out what your name means and spend some time reflecting on it. Do you feel it fits who you are and who God has called you to be? Prayerfully consider what name you feel

God might give you. Is there a new name that you would like to be called by? A friend of mine who was known for much of his life as Bill, decided to be called Will after he became a Christian, proclaiming that his will was to follow God. My name, Christine means "follower of Christ" which delighted me when I found out its meaning as I have spent most of my life seeking to be a true follower of Christ.

Creator God,
Who formed me
From the dust of the earth
And the substance of your being,
Thank you that you see me,
And know me by name.
Help me to remember
Your name for me,
And not allow the names of the world
To drown out your voice.
Help me to see others as you do,
To affirm their gifts and talents,
And recognize the names you give them,
Precious child, beloved of God,
Kin in the eternal family.
May I learn their names,
And treat them as brothers and sisters,
Worthy of the same love
With which you treat me.

December 16th — Paying Attention with St. Aidan

Listen to me, coastlands;
  pay attention, peoples far away.
The Lord called me before my birth,
  called my name when I was in my mother's womb.
(Isaiah 49:1 CEB)

There is joy in paying attention to our lives. I am contemplating that question as I sit in my quiet place listening to the birds sing and watching the mountains glow in the early morning light. Paying attention is about taking notice of ourselves, God, our neighbours, the earth on which we live and the circumstances in which we find ourselves.

Henri Nouwen writes: "The gift of discernment is the ability to hear and see from God's perspective and to offer that wisdom from above to others." He goes on to add: "Together, God's people ground me in the reality and wholeness of Christ and his church, holding me firm and safe in God's living embrace. God speaks regularly to us through people who talk to us about the things of God. Certain people become living signs that point us to God. Whether in life or in memory, the people God puts in our lives can help guide us and show us the way."[72]

I think that St. Aidan was one who knew how to pay attention in the way that Henri Nouwen describes and received much joy from it. Irish by birth, he was educated on Iona where he learned the value of prayer, study, self-discipline and generosity which shaped his ministry. While on Iona, another monk returned from a mission to Northumbria on the east coast of England frustrated and angry, saying that the people were unteachable. St. Aidan agreed to go in his place, convinced that to convert the people a gentle, humble and listening touch was necessary.

When he arrived he settled on Lindisfarne, later known as Holy Island, an isolated island that was and still is cut off from the mainland at high tide. It was a place he felt he could retreat to for solitude and prayer. Throughout his ministry, Aidan loved to walk among the people listening, learning and teaching. He encouraged everyone he met to be generous and merciful and was always aware of and quick to respond to the needs of the poor.

He often gave away the gifts he received. On one occasion for example, he was given a beautiful horse with royal trappings by King Oswald. However upon seeing a poor beggar off the road, he immediately gave the horse away. When the king heard of this, he questioned Aidan asking why he gave the horse away "Aren't there less valuable horses you could have given to the poor?" the king asked. Aidan responded "Is that foal more valuable to you than the poor child of God to whom I gave it?" The king pondered his words and suddenly unbuckled his sword and laid himself at Aidan's feet telling him that he would never again question what gifts of his were handed on to the children of God. Aidan lifted him up and embraced him with great joy.[73]

I have learned a lot about the joy of paying attention in the ways that Aidan did, using some of the techniques that I suspect he used. First, I have learned to take notice of God's world. Aidan, like many of the early Christian saints, believed that creation was translucent and the glory of God shone through. A raindrop, a ripe strawberry, even a broken branch reflect something of who God is. My own love of creation grows every year, and the beauty and the wonder of God's world fills me with awe. Unfortunately, especially in the winter it is easy to let go of this focus. I still need to take time to look and listen and touch, to allow the glory of God reflected in creation to seep into my being.

Second, I have learned to take notice of God's people. Aidan was very good at paying attention to the people in his path - not just the rich and the powerful like King Oswald, but the poor and the marginalized like the beggar he gave the horse to. All people are God's people, made in God's image to reflect who God is. Even the most broken people (and we are all broken people) can draw us closer to the God we love. Yet we easily listen to some and dismiss others. We pay attention to those we like or whose opinions we agree with and ignore or demonize others who think, look or worship differently. We sit in fellowship with those who make us comfortable and distance ourselves from those who make us uncomfortable.

In the Advent and Christmas story, God seems to delight in sending messengers from the margins. Like the shepherds, the lowliest of society whom Mary and Joseph seem to have welcomed in to see their baby. That they could be seen as Godly messengers bringing the joy of the angels' announcement with them and were accepted by Joseph's family is remarkable. Then there are the Magi, foreigners from afar, again unacceptable in Jewish society, yet welcomed in to see the Christ child.

Reflection

Who are you willing to listen to? Who do you ignore and not welcome into your life? Who will you allow God to speak through in unexpected and surprising ways? The more intentionally I take time and create space for these questions, the more I pay attention especially to those at the margins through whom God often speaks, the more joy I gain in my life. I also become more grateful for all the ordinary, mundane aspects of life, and the ordinary people who impact me.

Go outside and find a contemplative place to sit and be attentive to God's creation around you. Close your eyes and listen carefully. What does it feel like to pay attention in this way? What was your experience like? What emotions arise? How might you respond to God? Take some time today to grapple with these questions and to find the joy that God would have you enter into at this season.

Expect the unexpected,
Don't let it ruin your day.
Go with the flow,
Of broken plans,
And unfulfilled hopes.
Look for the silver linings,
And unanticipated blessings.
Embrace God's comfort,
Shown in the love of friends,
And care of strangers.

Relish the wonder of life.
Allow its hidden paths
To guide you into joy,
And shape who you will become.

December 17th — The Joy of A Vulnerable God

After the wise men left, a messenger of the Lord appeared to Joseph in a dream.
Messenger of the Lord *(to Joseph)**: Get up, take the child and His mother, and head to Egypt. Stay there until I tell you it is safe to leave. For Herod understands that Jesus threatens him and all he stands for. He is planning to search for the child and kill Him. But you will be safe in Egypt. So Joseph got up in the middle of the night; he bundled up Mary and Jesus, and they left for Egypt.* (Matthew 2:13,14 The Voice)

Several years ago I created an Advent garden with six words for me to meditate on during Advent. One of those words was vulnerable. We live in a world in which all of us feel vulnerable at times but our lives don't seem nearly as vulnerable as they would have been for the Celtic Christians we are learning about this Advent season. Not only did they face the vulnerability of winter food shortages, of wild beasts and bandits when they travelled but also, as the monasteries became rich and prosperous, of Viking raids.

The first blow of the raiders was against Lindisfarne, off the northeast coast of today's England. Alcuin, a noted scholar, lamented, "Behold the church of St. Cuthbert spattered with the blood of the priests of God, despoiled of all its ornaments." Two years later Vikings struck on the opposite coast, raiding the monastery on Iona. Norsemen sacked Iona again in 802, burning the monastery and in 806, they killed sixty-eight monks. By then, most of the monks had moved to Kells, in Ireland. In 825, another raid looking for Columba's reliquary, killed all the monks on the island. Raiders sacked Iona many more times over the next two centuries. The last assault was recorded in 987. I can't imagine living with this kind of vulnerability.

When I wrote the word vulnerable, however, it was Mary's vulnerability I thought of. Powerless and open to attack in a world that did not look favourably on unwed mothers. A member of a marginalized people on the edges of the Roman Empire. I thought too of the Mary-like people in our world today who are also vulnerable because of their powerlessness – those caught in the grip of poverty, abuse, racial & sexual discrimination, refugees, the disabled, those caught in the horrors of war. The list of the victims of powerlessness is so long it is overwhelming. And to that I add the vulnerability of our planet – 1 million species that might become extinct in the near future, the hottest year on record, a fire season that now in some parts of the world is 12 months long.

This too is overwhelming, but that I realize is what vulnerability is all about – feeling powerless in the face of power and wealth. And that is how many of us feel today. We are all feeling vulnerable as we face the uncertainties of the future and it's a hard place to be in. I think that many of the Celtic saints felt vulnerable in the same ways. Their future was probably even more uncertain than ours.

God too is vulnerable. Our Creator always comes to us in ways that open the possibility of attack, abuse, and woundedness. In fact that is very much the story of God revealed in Jesus Christ. An unexpected and vulnerable Messiah revealing an unexpected and vulnerable God. Why I wonder did the immense and magnificent Creator of the universe decide to be manifested in a child born at the margins of the empire, vulnerable not just to the usual scourges of diseases and poverty, but also to the possibility of death, even in his conception because his mother was unwed?

My impression of God as a rich and powerful leader faded over the last few years as images of the One who comes to us in powerlessness and vulnerability solidified. Not a ruler but a servant, not an authoritarian commander but a gentle leader, a companion and guide who is particularly concerned about the other vulnerable ones in our midst and who brings change not from the centres of power but from the margins where other vulnerable beings dwell.

As I wait during this season of Advent, I wait with joy for this vulnerable God and I feel hope well up within me. It's important, I believe, to live with a vision of hope that fills us with joy, a vision of God's better future in which all things are made new. Without a vision like this we will never strive to see our world changed and that is very much the vision that fills my heart as I look through Advent towards Christmas this year.

Reflection

During Advent, a canvas print of pregnant Mary and Elizabeth meeting sits on my desk. It was given to me by my good friend Tom Balke who photographed it on a visit to the Taize community several years ago. It speaks to me of the vulnerability as well as the hope and joy of both Mary and Elizabeth as they excitedly meet and share the delight of their respective pregnancies. Both of them are obviously pregnant with their babies outlined in their wombs. John leaps in Elizabeth's womb at his excitement.

It is hard for us to understand a powerful God who comes in such vulnerability, yet in this God we place our hope. Not only is God in the midst of our uncertainty, they are calling us into it. I find this very challenging. It is often in the margins of our lives, including our uncertainty, where we meet Jesus again and again. This is the God whose presence will one day fill our world bringing renewal and transformation.

The prayer below encourages me to ask: Where in this season of Celtic Advent am I waiting? How might God be speaking through this? What makes you feel vulnerable and uncertain at the moment? How do you respond to that vulnerability? Prayerfully ponder these questions and journal about your responses.

Today I wait,
My heart longing, yearning, aching
For the fulfillment of God's promises.
I wait
in hope, in expectation,
Trusting that which is not yet visible.
I will not despise the vulnerability,
Of God and God's beloved son,

By refusing to believe,
God's desire is to see all things made new.
I will not deny the wonder of a God,
Who created all things in goodness and delight,
And saw them worthy to be restored and made whole.
I wait,
For in Christ God's circle is complete.
What began in creation,
Finds its fulfillment in him.
I will not give up hope of the promise
For peace and justice and flourishing
Hidden in a vulnerable child,
Born in a manger.
Love will prevail.
God's light will shine
All will be made new.
Where do you see signs of our vulnerable God?
What signs of God's presence give you hope for the future?

Week Six —
Embracing Love

December 18th — Welcoming A Child with Celtic Mothers

Joseph went to be enrolled together with Mary, who was promised to him in marriage and who was pregnant. While they were there, the time came for Mary to have her baby. She gave birth to her firstborn child, a son, wrapped him snugly, and laid him in a manger, because there was no place for them in the guest room. (Luke 2: 5-7 CEB)

As the birth of Christ approaches and we make the final preparations to welcome him into our midst, our thoughts turn with love and joy, anticipation and delight towards his coming. What will he look like to us this Christmas? How will we welcome him? Will he seem like a stranger or a friend?

Henri Nouwen calls hospitality "the creation of a free and friendly space where we can reach out to strangers and invite them to become our friends…." He goes on to suggest that the most important guests, the most important strangers we get to entertain in our homes are our children. When they are born, we don't really understand who they are or who they will become. "They are guests we need to respond to, not possessions we are responsible for."[74]

Celtic mothers sang beautiful birth/baptism prayers to welcome their children after they were born. It is a wonderful, loving ritual that embraces this special newborn infant as a gift of God and a friend coming into our midst. I love the imagery of these prayers. I can imagine the mother gazing lovingly into the child's eyes. Then she would put three drops of water on the forehead of the newborn "the poor little infant, who has come home to us from the bosom of the everlasting Father" and softly sing this song of welcome while rocking her infant in her arms, caressing, reassuring, enfolding the child in her love and in the love of the Trinity. By the end of the prayer she knew that the Trinity was indwelling in her newborn child and that each member of the Sacred Three brought a different blessing and would play a different role in the child's life.[75]

The blessing of the Holy Three little love, be dower to thee,
Wisdom, Peace and Purity.

A few years ago, my nephew Matt and his wife Kass came from Australia with their 6-month-old baby Lucy to visit. They wanted to introduce us to this precious little one who had just become part of their family. We did everything possible to welcome this baby, this stranger whom we hoped would become a friend. We cleared out our guest room to create space for her crib. We rearranged our schedules so we could spend as much time with her as possible, often holding her in our arms, looking into her face, imprinting the beauty of her on our minds. We accepted her as she is now, not trying to change her into who we want her to become but seeking to identify and encourage her to develop the gifts God has placed within her.

We forget sometimes that Jesus too came as a baby and as a stranger into the midst of his family and community. He was an unwanted baby to many, born to an unwed mother, outside the bonds of convention and acceptability. Yet he was welcomed by his mother Mary with great excitement and delight. I can imagine her too rocking him in her arms, singing, caressing and praying for him. Also he was welcomed by Joseph as a part of his family. He too probably held this newborn child with love and affection, wondering what this child would become, praying that God's promises for him would be fulfilled.

What if we read life with the belief that all are welcome at God's table, strangers who God wishes to become friends just as Mary and Joseph befriended Jesus? What would it look like if I was willing to welcome every stranger as I welcomed my great niece and as I will welcome Jesus in a few day? There are so many who are strangers in our midst that are waiting for us to sit down and invite them to become friends, just as we invited little Lucy and her parents into our home and invited her to become a friend.

Reflection

How did you respond to the last newborn infant you were introduced to? Did you sing a song of welcome to this precious beloved one of God? What feelings and emotions welled up within you? Did this child feel like a friend or a stranger? What changes in behavior were you willing to make in order to get to know this child, accommodate its needs, help it feel welcome in your home? Visualize that encounter in your mind, reflect on it and write about it in your journal.

Now think about the last time you met a stranger – perhaps a homeless person on the street or a new member at your church. How did you welcome them as you would welcome a child? In what ways did you endeavor to turn this stranger into a friend? Consider using this prayer as a blessing for the new babies in your circle of friends.

The little drop of the Father
On thy little forehead, beloved one.
The little drop of the Son
On thy little forehead, beloved one.
The little drop of the Spirit
To aid thee from the Fays,
To shield thee from the host;
To keep thee from the gnome;
To shield thee from the spectre;
To keep thee from the Three,
To shield thee, to surround thee;
To save thee from the Three,
To fill thee with the graces;
The little drop of the Three
To lave thee with the graces. [76]

December 19th — Uncertainty of Waiting for Love

The angel replied, "The Holy Spirit will come over you and the power of the Most High will overshadow you. Therefore, the one who is to be born will be holy. He will be called God's Son. Look, even in her old age, your relative Elizabeth has conceived a son. This woman who was labeled 'unable to conceive' is now six months pregnant. Nothing is impossible for God." (Luke 2:35-37 CEB)

Celtic Christians knew a lot about waiting, especially at this time of the year, which was for them the darkest days of the year, with the winter solstice, the midpoint of winter, only a few days away. However, the darkness was not the focus of the season for the Celts but rather, the coming of the light and the knowledge that the light would overcome the darkness. They knew that these lengthening days were soon coming and waited in joyful expectation for the light both physical and spiritual to be reborn as the days began to lengthen once more.

It is only a few days until Christmas, and I am sure that the anticipation was growing and joy abounded especially amongst the children. They were getting ready for a twelve-day celebration of festivity and fun. There was the Yule log, the crowning glory of the feast, to cut down. It was first lit on Christmas Eve and hopefully would continue to burn not just through Christmas Day but throughout the whole season of Christmas. It often took a whole group of people to haul this important log home, sometimes with small children astride it. Once it arrived in the house, it was decorated with holly, ivy and other greenery. Last, it was sprinkled with a libation of cider or ale before being consigned to its fate upon the hearth. Musicians played and drinks flowed as it blazed up, filling the room with warmth, light and cheer. The whole household sat around it drinking whiskey, ale or wine, eating cake and telling jokes and stories. For a little while dark and cold were defeated, the specter of poverty, hunger and disease, too often unwelcome gifts of midwinter, were kept at bay outside the protective circle of the sun brought back to life.[77]

Tragically, in 1644, when parliament won the civil war in England, Scotland and Ireland, The Church of England was abolished and replaced by Calvinism and the Presbyterian system. Christmas festivities and displays of Christmas decorations were banned as frivolous and wasteful, a festival that threatened the very core of their Christian beliefs. All the fun was taken out of Christmas. Though this ban only lasted about 30 years in England, in Scotland the ban lasted 400 years, and was not officially lifted until 1958. I think this is what the beaver in C.S. Lewis's *The Lion, The Witch and the Wardrobe,* was referring too when he says that "it was always winter and never Christmas." The Celts had to wait a long time to celebrate again in the full festive spirit of the season.

Waiting is an integral and important part of the Biblical narrative too and God does a lot of it. At this stage of Advent, most of us feel that Christmas Day is coming very fast, and yet we know that once Christmas Day has passed, we will still be waiting and it seems so long, this in-between time between the promise and its final fulfillment.

The Eternal One's preparation for the birth of Jesus goes back before the beginning of time. God, whose very nature is love and life and light knew from the beginning of time that the coming of Jesus was necessary. It is written in the words of the prophets. According to astrologers it was even written in the stars. Our Creator, the ever present, ever loving One, has known the sorrow and the joy of preparation not just for 9 months, but throughout eternity. And the waiting for the fulfillment of the promise for wholeness and flourishing that will mark the return of Christ, is not over.

Are we willing to wait? Elizabeth waited most of her married life for the birth of a child. Now she was old and I suspect had almost abandoned her dream. Mary waited nine months for the birth of the child that the angel foretold would change the world. Then she waited throughout his life to see that dream fulfilled. Today we still wait for the completion of this dream to be fulfilled.

Abraham was not willing to wait as long as God wanted him to. He was too impatient for the child he had dreamed of for years. Sarah laughed because she no longer believed the promise of a child was possible. Joseph didn't think he should wait at all and arrogantly shared his dreams with his brothers.

How many others have dreamed God's dreams and then tried to fulfill them in their own way and at their own time? We know that it is dangerous for a pregnant woman to give birth before her time. She needs to wait 9 months before her baby is born. I am sure that Mary became very uncomfortable as the baby grew inside her. I am sure she longed for the birth and wished it would happen soon. However, I am also sure she was willing to wait because she knew that an early birth could mean complications and even death for both her and her child. I bet she did everything she could to keep the child growing within her healthy, in spite of her own discomfort.

How many of us laugh at God's promises like Sarah did because we feel we have already waited too long and no longer believe?

The garden teaches me important lessons about waiting. Seeds need time to germinate. Fruit and flowers need time to grow and mature. There are no shortcuts to the beauty and abundance that the garden promises, but the wait is worth it.
The Advent story encourages us to wait, to prepare, to hope for the promises of God's love yet to come.

Reflection

We don't like to wait, and we live in a world which tells us we should not have to. Do you have a dream that you have given up on because you were not willing to wait, and how long should we wait anyway before we stop believing in the promises of God to be fulfilled? How long before we turn our backs on God's seeming lack of response? We know how long it will be from a child's conception to its birth, and we want that kind of certainty about the promises of God. A timeline that says "this will be the day".

Close your eyes and prayerfully look back over your life. Is there a dream that you have given up on because you were not willing to wait? Is there one that was born prematurely and did not survive because of your impatience? Visualize these dreams and place them in God's hands. Is there a dream that God is nudging you to take up again as we journey through these last few days of Advent towards Christmas?

How long should we wait
Before we give up on a dream?
How long should we hope
Before we discard a promise?
How long God Almighty,
Before your dreams and promises
Become reality.
God, meet us in our waiting.
Abraham couldn't wait,
Joseph didn't want to.
Will we laugh in disbelief like Sarah?
Or will we sing with joy like Mary?
When God says:
Now is the time
For the impossible to be birthed.
God still waits,
And meets us in our waiting,
To fulfill the promises
Begun in Jesus' birth.
Come soon Prince of Peace
Bring our waiting to an end,
Come into our hurting world
Give birth to your new world
Of light and love and wholeness.

December 20th — Receive the Gifts of Christmas

The star they had seen in the east went ahead of them until it stood over the place where the child was. When they saw the star, they were filled with joy. They entered the house and saw the child with Mary his mother. Falling to their knees, they honored him. Then they opened their treasure chests and presented him with gifts of gold, frankincense, and myrrh. (Matthew 2:9-11 CEB)

For many years, Tom and I hosted an annual Open House just before Christmas. One of my favourite recipes for this event was Scottish shortbread. I made at least four batches each year for the open house and more for gifts to send to friends near and far. Some of our friends came to the Open house more for the shortbread than to see Tom and I. I only make shortbread at Christmas, a tradition well in keeping with my Scottish heritage which linked shortbread with the Yule season - Christmas to New Year's, called the Hogmanay. It was carried by "first-footers," those who visited from house to house in the wee hours of New Year's morning. For good luck this first footer should be a dark haired person — a tradition I know my grandmother rigorously adhered to. To be honest my favourite gifts at this time of year, are those that are home made, like my shortbread. They are usually made with much love and given with love, and infused with something of who I am, homemade gifts are part of the person who gives them.

A couple of years ago my friend Lilly Lewin hosted a Sacred Space Prayer Experience at a local coffee shop, Humphreys Street Coffee, in Nashville Tennessee that gives a beautiful perspective on the giving of gifts. For three days, Sacred Space was an open house for God and her gift to the community. People could pop in to create something in art, pray the stations or just sit and read a book or rest from the busyness of the season. The theme of the Sacred Space was RECEIVE THE GIFT. All the prayer stations were based around gifts and used bows, wrapping paper, and small gift packages as decorations or props to pray with. It was like a Montessori Church. It involved participation. Each station had something to do or experience. Like putting on baby lotion as a reminder to receive the gift of baby Jesus.

As people wrapped their gifts, Lilly invited Jesus to wrap them in his great love. She suggested we ask Jesus to help us truly feel his love and peace surrounding us like the paper surrounds the present. She provided several questions that really help us feel wrapped in God's love at this season. She suggested taking time, while we wrapped our presents: "Take time to be grateful for all the gifts of love we had experienced lately. Friends, family, things that have made you smile." As we stuck on the scotch tape, (sellotape), we were asked to consider what kept us stuck in our lives and in our relationship with Jesus? She then suggested we talk to him about these sticky things and allow Jesus to set us free! Bows and ribbons reminded her of celebrations and she asked us to consider what we celebrated this Advent. What things are we grateful for? Finally, she invited us to pray for the person the gift is for. As we write cards or gift tags, ask Jesus to help this person receive the Gift of God's great love this Christmas.[78]

Celtic saints were known for their generosity. One delightful story tells of a meeting between Kentigern of Glasgow (also known by the pet name Mungo) and Columba of Iona. They are said to have spent many hours together talking and when they got up to leave, exchanged gifts. Kentigern gave Columba his pastoral staff and Columba gave Kentigern his. Each of them then took the other's powerful emblem away with them.

Gift giving is an important part of Christmas, probably relating to the gifts of the magi to Christ after his birth. These three men, foreigners from a far country, came with very generous gifts for the Christ child. The sense of generosity that abounds at this time of year is wonderful to see, and the giving of gifts can be a deeply moving experience, especially when those gifts come from our hearts.

Reflection

When you open a gift during the holidays, consider what Gifts God is inviting you to open. What are the new and maybe even the unexpected Gifts God has for you this final week of Advent? Ask God to show you. Take time to notice.

Many of us are overwhelmed by the profusion of gifts passed around at Christmas. This year, try to view them from a new perspective. Use the gift packages you see, under the tree, in shops and even on tv commercials to remind you of all the gifts God has given you and to remind you of the greatest Gift...JESUS.

What Gifts are you looking for today?
What hopes, dreams, plans, prayers have you been waiting for, longing for,
Waiting for them to be fulfilled?
Consider & pray about what gifts you might receive today.

December is
the Season of Gifts...
The Season of both Giving and Receiving
Today you are invited to RECEIVE.
Today be open to Receiving ...
The Gift of Space and Time to slow down & be still.
The Gift of Hope for a world that often feels hopeless.
The Gift of Peace for a world filled with conflict.
The Gift of Light that comes to our darkness.
The Gift of a Baby King born in the messiness of life
to a teenage girl
The Gift of Emmanuel...God is with us![79]

December 21st — Brigid the Midwife of Mary

Since Joseph belonged to David's house and family line, he went up from the city of Nazareth in Galilee to David's city, called Bethlehem, in Judea. He went to be enrolled together with Mary, who was promised to him in marriage and who was pregnant. While they were there, the time came for Mary to have her baby. (Luke 2: 4-6 CEB)

Just before Christmas I set up our Nativity set. Where's the midwife I ponder as I get ready to celebrate the twelve days of Christmas? Mary's midwife isn't present in the nativity sets we use to decorate our homes during Advent and Christmas season, though evidently she often appears in Ancient Orthodox and Byzantine icons of the event.

While it's true that Luke doesn't mention the presence of a midwife in his account of the nativity, it's easy to imagine Mary attended by one, just as Jewish mothers had been for thousands of year. Like so many other figures in the gospel narrative, this midwife is never named, though Orthodox tradition calls her Salome. Sometimes she is depicted in the corner or background of icons of the manger scene. She might be preparing something for Mary, observing quietly, or giving Jesus his first bath!

Irish tradition says that it was Brigid of Kildare who somehow travelled through time and space to be with Mary and deliver this precious child and provide for his early needs. It is hard for us to believe that Brigid was indeed transported back in time to perform this important role, but to the Irish, Brigid abides in eternity. They believed that her caring, compassionate heart was learned at the manger. She is seen as the companion of the Holy Family, Mary's trusted friend and helper, a kind and faithful nurse to Jesus.[80] This tradition continues today in Ireland, Scotland and Wales, reminding us that Jesus is always being born in our midst.

It's probable that Mary and Joseph arrived in Bethlehem several days before Jesus was born. There is no sense of urgency in today's scripture, no indication that Mary was already in labour when they arrived. It is probable that Mary and Joseph had ample time to prepare for her delivery and to seek out a local midwife. It is even likely that some of Joseph's female relatives were there too. After all this was his home town and whether Jesus was born in a cave where animals were kept, or in a family home, as I suspect, in a culture as hospitable as this they would not have been left to birth the baby on their own.

This woman, reminds me of my early days as a physician in New Zealand when I too helped to bring babies into the world. It was the most precious experience imaginable, one that I never tired of. So I close my eyes and imagine myself transported back 2,000 years to give birth to that special child. After all if Brigid can travel through time I should be able to as well. I imagine myself comforting Mary as she cries out in the pangs of childbirth. I imagine listening for Jesus's first breath, and hear him give his first cry. I bath him, gently wiping off the blood and fluids of his passage through the birth canal. Then I lay him on his mother's breast, enthralled by her radiant smile and I beckon Joseph to her side.

It is hard to believe, as we think of this tiny child, so rudely and violently expelled into the world, and now lying quietly in all his vulnerability and dependency, that he is indeed the promised saviour, the son of God. Like I did after each delivery, did the midwife look at his tiny body in awe and wonder, filled with the joy and delight of helping to bring to birth a child in whom the divine spark was obviously present. Did she go away changed just as the shepherds and the wise men were changed by their encounter? Did she cherish the face of this child in her mind aware that he was special and would transform the world?

Reflection

We have not all had children, or experienced the joy of delivering babies like I have, but most of us know people who have. Speak to a doula, midwife, doctor or nurse who has helped in the delivery of a baby. Or speak to your parents about your own birth or the birth of one of your siblings. What was that experience like for them? What emotions did it stir? How has it changed their view of God and of the world? Take time to reflect on what you learn. Close your eyes and imagine yourself in their position, holding a newborn baby in your arms. How do you think it would change you?

A newborn babe
brings light to the house
warmth to the hearth
and joy to the soul.
For wealth is family
family is wealth.
May strong arms hold you
Caring hearts tend you
And may love await you at every step.
May you bring light to the home,
warmth to the heart
Joy to the soul
And love to the lives you touch.[81]

December 22nd — Holy Mothering of St. Non

She gave birth to her firstborn child, a son, wrapped him snugly, and laid him in a manger, because there was no place for them in the guest room. (Luke 2:7 CEB)

Much beloved by the people of Wales, Saint Non was the mother of St. David, the patron saint of that country. Because of her strong mothering and caring, nurturing ways with David, which led to a strong church in Wales, Non is seen as a holy mother. In fact she is known as the holy mother of the Welsh church.

Non's story is not an easy one. She was raped by the king of the region and in this act of violence, David was conceived. According to tradition, the earth responded to David's conception and two standing stones came out of the earth, one at her head and one at her feet. Creation itself recognized that a saintly child would come from her womb. Non continued to live a holy life and prayed and trusted that the child within her would be a gift for her people.

On one occasion during her pregnancy, she entered a church hungry for the word of God. The preacher immediately lost the ability to preach and could not do so until she left. It was obvious that the child within her was a Godly child whose presence was more powerful than the preacher's voice.

On another occasion, a local ruler, learning from the prophesies of his druids that Non's son would rule over his realm, kept watch intending to kill the newborn baby. When the time came for David's birth, Non was walking along the cliffs above the seas. A fierce storm broke as she began her labour, and hail and rain fell all around her, protecting her from the tyrant's pursuit. At the place where she lay, a brilliant light shone and no rain fell. The stone on which she leaned her hands in the midst of her labour was marked with imprints of her hands. She birthed David in the wild solitude of the cliffs above the sea. Once he was born, a spring erupted from the ground and pure water flowed, responding to Non's faithfulness and courage.[82]

After David was born he was sent to live with a foster family in a neighbouring region, a common practice with children from prominent families in Ireland at that time. Non went to Cornwall and founded a church at Altarnon which was close to a holy well known for its healing properties. A beautiful Celtic cross still stands by the church gate.

Non was a woman of great courage and faith, a faith she passed on to her son who was known to treat others always with respect and kindness. How hard it must have been to leave him in the hands of others. Yet she demonstrated faithful mothering throughout her pregnancy, through her labour and David's birth and fostering and wrenched herself away to go to Cornwall.

As I read this story I could not help but think of how hard it must have been for the mothering instincts of God to let go of Jesus and give him into the hands of a human mother to raise. What an incredible level of trust and humility from the creator of the Universe. Mary's pregnancy from Jesus' conception til his birth was fraught with danger, God must have frequently felt like intervening to make things easier. In spite of this danger, in spite of the fact that life carrying the son of God was a challenging calling that disrupted her whole life, the impression we get is of a loving mother, concerned for the welfare of her son more than for herself.

Reflection

Who, apart from your biological mother, has been a mother to you? Sit for a few minutes with your eyes closed and reminisce in your mind about those who have mothered you throughout your life. When you open your eyes do some journalling about these women who have played such a special place in your life. You might like to write them letters as well.

Close your eyes again and consider when you have been aware of the mother heart of God. When did you know God's comforting, nurturing presence? Sit and imagine yourself climbing onto God's lap and into the holy embrace.

God with a mother's heart,
You gather us as your children.
You comfort and hold us in your warm embrace.
When we hurt your arms enfold us.
When we are afraid your wings protect us.
When we are hungry you feed us with the bread of life.
God with a mother's heart,
Your love surrounds and supports us,
In good times and in tough,
In the midst of joy and pain,
Always and everywhere.
You will never leave nor abandon us.
God eternal and loving one,
God with a mother's heart,
We thank you this day,
For your mothering love.

December 23rd — St. Hilda Mother of the Church

God was like an eagle hovering over its nest,
overshadowing its young,
Then spreading its wings, lifting them into the air,
teaching them to fly. (Deuteronomy 32:11 The Message)

St. Hilda is venerated as an icon for Godly Wisdom - the rich nurturing and maternal dimension that is within God and which God has placed in the created order. She was an amazing leader who founded a double monastery at Whitby. The Venerable Bede records that Aidan, Caedmon and the other brothers loved Hilda heartily for her innate wisdom, that her prudence was such that she was consulted by many people from different walks of life, encouraging and counseling them so that all those who knew her called her mother. Hilda had exceptional insight born of a mother's compassion.[83]

Hilda is often remembered for her gift of encouragement to a young uneducated herdsman by the name of Caedmon who lived near Whitby. When songs and stories were shared in the evenings Caedmon would slip out, embarrassed because he thought he had no ability to sing. One night he had a dream and heard a voice saying "Sing something to me." He confessed he could not sing and the voice said "Sing of creation." Suddenly Caedmon began to sing beautiful poetry praising God's gift of creation. The next morning he was able to share this with mother Hilda, who recognizing his gift encouraged him to take holy vows. He became a monk and a singer and today is known as the first English poet.

Our world is dominated by images of God as father, the images of the nurturing, caring God who holds us, grieves with us and laughs with us are less common. Yet today, as I think about the story of God, and especially our journey through this last week of Advent towards the birth of Christ, what strikes me is how mother-like God's whole involvement with humankind is and today I imagine our Creator hovering like a mother hen over Mary as she waits for her child, God's beloved child, to be born.

In the beginning God reaches down into the soil, this warm, dark, protective womb like place where life begins, sculpts and fashions humankind, breathes on us and gives birth to us. Deuteronomy 32:10-18 is one of my favourite maternal images of God – first as one who embraces us with affection and comfort, then as an eagle who hovers protectively over her eaglet as it learns to fly, and finally as one who gives us good things to eat. Sadly this passage ends with God admonishing the Israelites for forgetting this nurturing, loving, caring mother heart: "You ignored the Rock who bore you and forgot the God who gave birth to you."

Unfortunately the church has not done justice either to these mothering images of God or to the women who helped shape its foundations and carried it through the centuries. Over the last few weeks we have met several of those women who like Mary and Elizabeth responded to the call of God on their lives and helped to shape the story of God. Like Mary and Elizabeth they were brave and courageous, often in spite of the discouragement or even adversity they experienced at the hands of the men around them. As our journey through Advent draws to a close, we realize that it is so often the women who take centre stage in this amazing story, often revealing the mother heart of a God who wishes to birth in all of us the characteristics of the Christ child born into our human world two thousand years ago.

Reflection

Read through the responsive reading below which focuses on some of the most beautiful images of the mothering heart of God in the Bible. Imagine yourself as one of those who was granted the privilege to help mother the Christ child as he entered our world - Mary and Elizabeth, Joseph's family, women in the caravan to Bethlehem and then later into

Egypt. We have no idea how many were involved in mothering Jesus and enabling this special child to become who God intended him to be. Which of these women catches your attention? Consider writing a note of gratitude to them for their mothering care of Jesus.

Today we thank God for the gift of mothers and mothering around the world.
As one whom a mother comforts, so I will comfort you – Isaiah 66:13. (RSV)
Gentle, patient God, thank you for your tender care.
Can a mother forget the baby at her breast
and have no compassion on the child she has borne?
Though she may forget,
I will not forget you! Isaiah 49:15 (NIV)
Loving, caring God thank you for your compassionate care.
But I have calmed and quieted myself,
I am like a weaned child with its mother;
like a weaned child I am content. Psalm 131:2 (NIV)
Protecting, embracing God thank you for your nurturing care.
How often have I longed to gather your children together, as a hen gathers her chicks under her wings… Matthew 23:37 (NIV)
Comforting, warmhearted God thank you for your gentle care.
God was like an eagle hovering over its nest,
overshadowing its young,
Then spreading its wings, lifting them into the air,
teaching them to fly. (Deuteronomy 32:11 The Message)
Ever present, sustaining God thank you for your enduring care.
I have cared for you since you were born. Yes, I carried you before you were born. (Isaiah 46:3 NLT)
Sustaining, all sufficient God thank you for your satisfying care.
I will be your God throughout your lifetime—
until your hair is white with age. I made you, and I will care for you. I will carry you along and save you. (Isaiah 46:4 NLT)
Faithful, providing God thank you for mothers and their love,
Everlasting and eternal One, thank you for your mothering love.[84]

December 24th — A Celtic Creche

The Word became flesh and blood,
and moved into the neighbourhood.
We saw the glory with our own eyes,
the one-of-a-kind glory,
like Father, like Son,
Generous inside and out,
true from start to finish. (John 1:14, The Message)

Of all the customs and traditions of Christmas, the creche or nativity set is my favorite. As a child, I remember my parents would have us slowly create the scene during the season of Advent. First, we set up the stable, and then over time, my brothers and I added a cow, a sheep and shepherd, and then an angel. The last week of Advent, Mary and Joseph took their places. The Three Kings were set up somewhere else in the house as they made their slow and solemn journey to Bethlehem. On Christmas Eve, a votive candle was lit and placed in the scene, symbolizing Christ's divinity. And then, finally on Christmas Day, the baby Jesus made his entrance, lying in the manger at the center of it all.

We were enacting that the Incarnation, God-with-us, entered into life in a very concrete and material way. As the Gospel of John writes, "And the Word became flesh and dwelt among us." (John 1:14) Or, in Eugene Peterson's paraphrase, "God put on flesh and blood and moved into our neighborhood." (The Message) That is a picture of a God who wants to get close to us. Think of God moving in as your next-door neighbor!

In fact, God is revealed in our neighbourhoods and in our homes, in one another and in creation. Celtic Christian imagination brings this point home, literally. It has been said that the genius of Celtic spirituality is its ability to fuse together the unique time and place of Christ's birth in

Bethlehem with our own specific present. It teaches us that Bethlehem can become present wherever we are.[85]

To illustrate that point, Patrick Thomas, a Welsh author and an Anglican priest, has written that in Welsh nativity scenes of the 19th and 18th centuries, whether it is a painting or a figurine set, a washerwoman, or laundress accompanies Mary, Joseph and Jesus at the manger. What a wonderful and beautiful thought, that God so loved the Holy Family that someone was sent to do the laundry!

On a more serious note, for the Welsh, God enters into the timeless story of the Holy Family by introducing a contemporary figure that they would recognize from their own culture–a working-class woman. It is interesting because a working-class woman of that period had about the same status as the shepherds did in Biblical times. One might romanticize shepherds but not working-class women. The Welsh people really understood who it was the Christ came for – the poor among their own communities. I love the Celtic understanding that there need not be a division nor a separation between the rich and poor, the divine and human, the spiritual and material, the sacred and ordinary, the real and imagined, this time and former times. To illustrate the last point, in the Irish tradition, there is a tradition that St. Brigid accompanied the Holy Family as the midwife, never mind the degrees of centuries' separation!

Intrigued by the Welsh tradition of bringing our lives into the nativity story, I engage in sacred play as part of my prayer. Over the years I have had a variety of nativity sets and I tend to favor indigenous ones. One of my favorite sets that I will use this year is from Africa. As I contemplated on how Christ is being born in my life this holy season, images of creation "danced in my head." During the pandemic, I learned to pray and worship outdoors. I am grateful for my prayer time in nature.

This year, my nativity scene will include not only the Celtic expression of the elements of earth, air, wind, and fire; but it will also include more friends of the animal kingdom. In addition to the donkey and sheep, as I placed my turtle, my quail and my owl in the scene, I also gave thanks for St. Francis. He of course created the first living creche by bringing in sheep, a donkey and a real live baby into a church on Christmas Eve, centuries ago. St. Francis and many of the Celtic saints would appreciate a more inclusive representation of the animals at any manger scene, I am sure. And as an aside, in the movie, "Love Actually" a school Christmas pageant in England included two lobsters at the birth of Jesus! That feels like the Celtic imagination and inspiration jumping into the culture of our day. And it is good! It is another indication that Christ was born for all.

That a laundress accompanies the Holy Family in Welsh art means that the Holy Family and Christ accompanies us in all our life tasks as well. So, I wonder, how is Christ being born in your life or in your children's and grandchildren's lives? Who might stand with the Christ child and stand in for you at the manger this Christmas season? Might you find a creative way to illustrate that reality in your home so that your household nativity scene reflects your understanding of how God is among us now?

Reflection

Perhaps, imagining being at the birth of Christ with the help of this meditation will spark your creativity:

"I open the stable door. I kneel before the infant. I worship with the shepherds. I adore the Christ child. I give my love with Mary and Joseph. I wonder at the Word made flesh. I absorb the love of God. I sing glory with the angels. I offer my gifts with the wise men; I have come from a land afar. I receive the living Christ. I hold Him in my hands. I go on my way rejoicing, glorifying and praising God."[86]

For to us a Child is born. Let us rejoice and give thanks for the many ways that Christ is born again in our lives!

Thank you God Almighty,
For your light that circles us,
When all seems dark and we are in despair.
Thank you God our Creator,
For your love that circles us,
When our world seems full of violence and hatred.
Thank you God our Comforter,

For your presence that circles us,
When we feel lost and alone.
Thank you God for you.[87]

Christmas —

Christ Born in our

Midst

December 25th — Christmas All Year Long

For unto us a child is born, to us a child is given,
And the government will be on his shoulders.
And he will be called Wonderful Counsellor,
Mighty God, Everlasting Father, Prince of Peace. (Isaiah 9:6 NIV)

Today we come to the end of our journey through Advent. Christ is born. Emanuel, God with us, not just in a distant land, but here, now in every day and every way, in every part of us. We hear the rejoicing of the cosmos, hope for a world transformed and a creation renewed. We drink in the wonder of it and sit in awe of what the birth of this child means not just for me or you, not just for humankind, but for the whole of God's creation.

It is this kind of God who invites us now to begin another journey beyond Christmas and into a new way of being.

For Celtic Christians as well as for many other traditions, Christmas was a 12-day celebration of festivity and fun. I relish Christmas and was absolutely delighted when I discovered that it is not meant to be a single day, but a whole season from Christmas Day until The Eve of Epiphany. It gives us time to reflect on all we have learned and where we want to go from here. I love that this season covers New Year's Day, that time when most of us attempt to make resolutions for the new year, as I feel these resolutions should flow out of our Advent journey and the new revelations we received along the way.

For most of us, Christmas is a season of many moods – of intense joy and celebration as we welcome the Christ child. Of despair and disbelief as we read about the massacre of the innocents in Bethlehem. Of dreaming and hope as we plan a new way forward. All of these are woven together in cords of love and life poured out by a compassionate God who we remember during these days, as the one who reached down and entered human history in an amazing way. Now it is time to join with our incredible God in the work that Jesus began. In the midst of this busy and at times overwhelming season, it is important to build in times of pause into your life. How might you carve out even a few minutes for reflection?

During Advent, we travelled with Mary and Joseph and their companions towards Christmas, supported, guided and surrounded by the Celtic saints. We entered the story of a very human, young woman living a perilous life at the fringes of the Roman Empire. We also entered the stories of brave men and women from Scotland, Ireland and Wales who kept the flame of Christ's love during the dark ages of Europe.

Now our focus shifts and it is time for us to both get into action and spend time in reflection. In her beautiful book *The Art of Advent,* Jane Williams says "This one act of God redefines so much". Even God-self is redefined she tells us. "God who is, by definition, beyond human knowledge, comes to be God with us, Emmanuel."[88] We still have trouble getting our heads around that, especially when we watch Jesus condemn the priests and teachers for their rigid, self-serving views of God. Like them we often try to push God away into a distant heavenly realm disconnected from this earth. It is hard to grasp that God comes into our world in vulnerability, championing the rights of the poor, healing the outcasts and comforting the widows. We want to hide from this kind of God, just as Adam and Eve hid in the Garden. But God is indeed with us in healing, comfort and love, with justice, mercy and generosity, in so many ways that it is hard for us to comprehend and asks us to join this new journey.

"This act of God redefines power. It takes all the might of the creator of the universe to enter into creation and become the opposite of God. It takes shocking force to absorb hatred and violence and death and turn it into love, peace and life."[89] It is this kind of God that we met on our pilgrimage with the Celtic saints - a God who is vulnerable, not powerful. A God who sides with those at the margins, rather than emperors and high priests. A God who stands up for justice especially for the marginalized. A God who heals, and feeds and cares for all the vulnerable ones - human and animal - of our world.

What a message of hope for today. God with us – here, now in every day and every way. It is this kind of God who invites us to continue to journey beyond Christmas and into a new way of being. We are invited to join the rejoicing of the cosmos, and we hear the rejoicing of the cosmos, hope for a world transformed and a creation renewed. We drink in the wonder of it and sit in awe of what the birth of this child means not just for me, not just for humankind, but for the whole of God's creation.

Reflection

Take time during the Christmas season for a mini retreat to help you discern the path ahead. Draw aside to a quiet place, for a few minutes, an hour or a day, and prayerfully seek God's help in designing the next stage of your journey.

Read back through the notes you took and the doodles, sketches and artwork you created during Advent. What shimmers for you with a sense of divine light and the whisper of God saying "This is the path, walk in it." What were the most compelling lessons you learned from Columba, Brigid, Patrick and Hilda and the many others we met on this journey?

What has been redefined for you as a result of your pilgrimage through Advent with the Celtic saints? What places and situations make it hard for you to believe that God is with you today? How has your journey through Advent helped you recognize God in these hard places? What new things did you learn about God and God's love for all creation?

Invite God to speak to you through the journey you took during Advent. What are the next steps you feel prompted to take? When would you like to reread your notes and reflections again? In six weeks, at the beginning of Lent? Mark that time on your calendar now.

Let us go forth today,
In the love of our Creator,
In the strength of our Redeemer,
In the power of our Sustainer,
In the fellowship of witnesses
From every tribe and nation

and culture.
Those who are present,
Those from the past,
Those who are yet to come.
Let us go forth today,
United with the Sacred Three,
In harmony with the Holy One,
Compassion in our hearts,
Gratitude in our thoughts,
Generosity in our deeds,
Justice as our passion.
Let us go forth today
Carrying God's image
Into our hurting world.

Acknowledgements

This book has been a very quick but satisfying endeavor, three months from the time I felt the spirit of God prompt me to embark on it until its completion. Self publishing is never an easy process, and not something that can be accomplished in isolation. Like the Celtic saints of old I feel that I have never walked alone. I have many wonderful companions with me along the journey.

Celtic Advent: Following An Unfamiliar Path would never have happened without my husband Tom who awakened my interest in Celtic Spirituality many years ago and reminisced with me as I collected stories of visits to Iona, Lindisfarne and Ireland. We too have followed an unfamiliar path, and one of the privileges of our lives has been the joy of travelling together to many parts of the world, nourishing our faith as we learned from our experiences, the people we encountered and God's good earth that we travelled through. Without Tom's companionship and the many ways he has cheered me on, this book would never have been written.

I am also grateful for my good friend Tom Balke who read through each reflection, sharing stories, making comments, and corrections as I wrote. His input enriched the book in many ways. His enthusiasm and encouragement were essential to me as I travelled from conception to birth of this book. He has been a very true and special spiritual guide for me along the way.

I am also blessed to have a very able assistant, Melissa Kelly, who embarked on the detailed editorial work that I always hate to do. She added commas, and citations, gave advice on formatting and went the extra mile to bring the project to completion.

I am grateful as well for Hilary Horn for her design work that contributed a professional touch to the book.

Last but not least I am grateful for those on Substack and Facebook who commented and motivated me to move forward. Their support too has made this book possible.

About the Author

Christine Aroney-Sine is a contemplative activist, passionate gardener, author, and liturgist, inspired by Celtic Christian spirituality. She posts on Substack, and is the founder and facilitator of the contemplative blog Godspacelight, which grew out of her passion for creative spirituality, gardening and sustainability. She hosts The Liturgical Rebels, a podcast for spiritual seekers no longer comfortable with traditional approaches to Christian religious observances but looking for new practices and approaches with which to connect to the divine. She facilitates workshops on contemplative and creative spiritual practices, and spirituality and gardening.

Christine trained as a physician in Australia, practiced in New Zealand and developed and directed the healthcare ministry for Mercy Ships. Her work took her to every continent except Antarctica.

Her latest book is *The Gift of Wonder: Creative Practices For Delighting in God*. She also self published several books, a bit of a hobby for her. These include: *Digging Deeper: the Art of Contemplative Gardening* (2022) *Rest in the Moment: Reflections for Godly Pauses* (2016), and *Return to Our Senses: Reimagining How We Pray* (2012)

You can connect to her on
Substack, https://christinesine.substack.com/
The Liturgical Rebels, https://liturgicalrebels.buzzsprout.com
Godspacelight, https://godspacelight.com
twitter https://twitter.com/ChristineSine or
Facebook https://www.facebook.com/christine.sine
Instagram: https://www.instagram.com/christine.sine/
Pinterest: https://www.pinterest.com/christinesine/
Youtube: https://www.youtube.com/user/Christinesine

Endnotes

[1] John Macquarrie *Paths in Spirituality, (London SCM Press, 1972) 123*

[2] John Newman, *Journeys with Celtic Christians,* (Abingdon Press, Nashville 2015) 27

[3] Jan Blencowe, *Celtic Advent, A Little Bit Longer, A Little Bit Wider,* https://janblencowe.com/celtic-advent-a-little-bit-longer-a-little-bit-wilder/

[4] Ian Bradley, *Colonies of Heaven: Celtic Christian Communities, Live the Tradition,* (Northstone Publishing, Kelowna, BC, Canada 2000) 5-6

[5] *Christine Sine*

[6] Jean McLachlan Hess *Journey to the Manger with Patrick and Friends* (Jean McLachlan Hess, 2015) 3

7 David Cole, Celtic Advent: *40 Days of Devotions to Christmas,* (The Bible Reading Fellowship, Abingdon, UK, 2018) 55, Kindle

8 *Rodney Newman, Journeys with Celtic Christians,* 70

9 Edward C Sellner, *Wisdom of the Celtic Saints, (*Ave Maria Press, Notre Dame, IN) 23

10 Sellner, Wisdom of the Celtic Saints, 23

11 Arne Bakken - *Pilgrimages Past and Present ,19*

12 The Prayer of St. Brendan - author unknown

13 Attributed to Archbishop Emeritus Desmond Tutu adapted from an original prayer by Sir Francis Drake.

14Sellner, Wisdom of the Celtic Saints, *93*

15 Translated into English by Irish linguist and journalist, Mary Byrne and later adapted into verse, by Eleanor Hull

16 *Rodney Newman,* Journeys With Celtic Christians, *19*

17 *https://www.taize.fr/en*

[18] *santiago-compostela.net/*

[19] Adapted from Lilly Lewin - *Taking Time for Pilgrimage* _https://godspacelight.com/ freerangefriday-taking-time-for-pilgrimage/_ Used with permission

[20] Adapted from an ancient prayer that comes at the end of the Pilgrim Mass said along the Camino De Santiago. *https://www.caminodesantiago.me/community/threads/a-pilgrims-prayer-to-st-james.71693/*

[21] Christine Pohl, *Making Room: Recovering Hospitality as a Christian Tradition* (Wm B Eerdmans Publishing, Grand Rapids, Mich, 1999) 6

[22] *Ancient Celtic rune of hospitality.*

[23] *Adapted from Robert Van de Weber, Celtic Fire,* (Doubleday New York, NY, 1990) *66*

[24] *Adapted from the Celtic Psaltery* _https://www.gutenberg.org/files/14232/14232-h/ 14232-h.htm #Page_20_

[25] *J Philip Newell , Christ of the Celts* (Jossey Bass, San Francisco CA, 2008) 50, 51

[26] *Carmina Gadelica, 45*

[27] John Philip Newell, *Sacred Earth, Sacred Soul: Celtic Wisdom for Reawakening What Our Souls Know and Healing the Earth, 32.*

[28] *John Philip Newell, The Book of Creation* (Paulist Press, Mahwah, New Jersey) xvii

[29]*John Philip Newell, Sacred Earth Sacred Soul, 36*

[30] *https://saintsbridge.org/2013/12/17/celts-to-the-creche-pelagius/*

[31] Yonatan Neril, Leo Dee: *Eco Bible Volume 1 An Ecological Commentary on Genesis and Exodus* (The Interfaith Center for Sustainable Development, 2020) *28*

[32] *Ancient Celtic prayer attributed to St. Brigid*

[33] Adapted from *John Philip Newell, Sacred Earth, Sacred Soul, 98,99*

[34] *https://en.wikipedia.org/wiki/Douglas_Hyde*

[35] Alexander Carmichael, *Carmina Gadelica; Hymns and incantations (*Flores Press, Edinburgh, 1992) 260.

[36] *Is This the Most Extreme Baptism,* BBC video _https://youtu.be/saLJNsKuabs? si=MboZww-xMSx-AEUE_

[37] Sellner, *Wisdom of the Celtic Saints,* 79

[38] Sellner, *Wisdom of the Celtic Saints,* 79

[39] *Adapted from:* Ray Simpson, *Hilda of Whitby a Spirituality for Now ,* (The Bible Reading fellowship, abingdon, UK 2014) 86

[40] *Carmina Gadelica, 241*

[41] Mary C. Earle and Sylvia Maddox , *Holy Companions: Spiritual Practices from the Celtic Saints.* (Moorehouse Publishing, Harrisburg PA 2004) 87

[42] *Adapted from Earle and Maddox, Holy Companions 87*

43 For a comprehensive discussion of shalom see Walter Brueggeman, Living Towards a Vision: Biblical Reflections on Shalom, (New York: United Church Press, 1976).

44 Walter Brueggeman, Living Toward a Vision, 16.

[45] Sellner, *Wisdom of the Celtic Saints,* 93

[46] *John O'Donahue, Anam Cara,* (Ava Maria Press, Notre Dame IN, 1993), *15*

[47] *I owe this prayer, found in The Poem Book of the Gaels, by Eleanor Hull, to Esther de Waal The Celtic Way of Prayer, 39*

[48] *Carmina Gadelica I, 25 quoted from Esther De Waal The Celtic Way of Prayer, 76*

[49] Esther de Waal, *The Celtic Way of Prayer - The Recovery of the Religious Imagination.* (Doubleday new York NY, 1997) 38

[50] *Adapted from Earle and Maddox, Holy Companions, 33-35*

[51] *Ray Simpson, Soul Friendship: Celtic Insights into Spiritual Mentoring,* (Hodder and Stoughton, London UK 1999) 3

[52] *John O'Donahue,* Anam Cara, *13*

[53] *John O'Donahue, Anam Cara, 23*

[54] *Mary DeJong ,Rewilding Wheel https://www.waymarkers.net/blog/2020/9/21/rewilding-wheel-seven-directions-prayer*

[55] This reflection is adapted from Mary DeJong's Caim circling prayer. *https://www.waymarkers.net/blog/2017/09/14/rewilding-prayer-how-caim-invites-protection-for-all-of-creation Used with permission.*

[56] *Adapted from Around a Thin Place,* Jane Bentley and Neil Paynter (Wild Goose Publications Glasgow Scotland 2011) 79,80

[57] Christine Valters Paintner, *The Love of Thousands : How Angels, Saints and Ancestors Walk with Us Towards Holiness.* (Sorin Books Notre Dame, IN 2023) 2

[58] Esther de Waal (Ed) *; The Celtic Vision: Prayers and Blessings from the Outer Hebrides,* (St. Bede's Publications, Petersham, Massachusetts, 1988) 160

[59] Adapted from Robert van der Weber, *Celtic Fire,* 117

[60] Dr Suzanne Simard *The Mother Project, https://mothertreeproject.org/wp-content/uploads/2020/01/the-mother-tree_the_word_for_world_is_still_forest.pdf*

[61] *Adapted from Sellner, Wisdom of the Celtic Saints 83*

[62] This blessing is adapted from Journey to Bethlehem Christmas Eve Meal by Catherine Wilson. h*ttps://www.focusonthefamily.ca/content/what-are-you-doing-on-christmas-eve-try-a-journey-to-bethlehem-meal*

[63] *For an excellent explanation of the image of Mary with the Christ Child in the Book of Kells https://youtu.be/qtQAsvUiwPg?si=izDzbHjNpddZ8vrl*

[64] *View the Book of Kells online here https://digitalcollections.tcd.ie/concern/works/hm50tr726*

[65] *John O'Donahue, The Invisible Embrace of Beauty, (Harper Perennial, New York, NY 2004) 19*

[66] *John O'Donahue, The Invisible Embrace of Beauty, 84.*

[67] *For more information about He Qi, https://www.heqiart.com/*

[68] *For more information about Kelly Latimore visit his website https://kellylatimoreicons.com/ or join him on Instagram https://www.instagram.com/kellylatimoreicons/*

[69] *Prayer found in the ruins of ancient Columban chapel near St. Columba's birthplace at Garten Lough, Co. Donegal.*

[70] *Daniel Taylor - In Search of Sacred Places: Looking for Wisdom on Celtic Holy Islands (Bog Walk Books, 2005)*

[71] *Daniel Taylor n Search of Sacred Spaces 37*

[72] Henri Nouwen, *Discernment: Reading the Signs of Daily Life,* (HarperOne, New York, NY 2013) 81.

[73] *Adapted from, Wisdom of the Celtic Saints, 52*

[74] Henri Nouwen, *Reaching Out: The Three Movements of the Spiritual Life* (Doubleday, New York NY, 1986) 79

[75] Adapted from Esther de Waal, *The Celtic Way of Prayer, 40-42*

[76] *Carmina Gadelica III, 7*

[77] Mara Freeman, *Kindling the Celtic Spirit: Ancient Traditions to Illumine Your Life Throughout the Seasons.* (Harper SanFrancisco, San Fransisco, 2001) 356

[78] *Adapted from Lilly Lewin - Receive the Gift https://godspacelight.com/50460/ Used with permission.*

[79] *Reflection and prayer from Lilly Lewin - Receive the Gift. https://godspacelight.com/50460/ Used with permission.*

80 Earle and Maddox, Holy Companions, 21

[81] This prayer is adapted from several ancient Celtic prayers for the newborn. Origin of each is unknown.

[82] *Adapted from Earle and Maddox, Holy Companions 28, 29*

[83] Ray Simpson, *Hilda of Whitby ,* 108

[84] *https://godspacelight.com/biblical-maternal-images-of-god/ The original post contains a video of the responsive reading as well as the written version.*

[85] *Patrick Thomas as quoted in A Holy Island Prayer Book by Ray Simpson,* (Morehouse Publishing; 1st edition November 1, 2002) 54

[86] David Adam , *The Open Gate*, 78

[87] *A Celtic Creche by The Rev. Elaine Breckenridge mother elaine@comcast.net a retired Episcopal priest residing on Camano Island, Washington. https://godspacelight.com/a-celtic-creche/ - used with permission.*

[88] Jane Williams, *The Art of Advent: A Painting a Day from Advent to Epiphany* (SPCK, London, UK 2018) 100

[89] Jane Williams, *The Art of Advent , 100*

Made in the USA
Columbia, SC
06 December 2024